Kathy MacMannis
Rag Wool Appliqué

- Easy to Sew
- Use Any Sewing Machine
- Quilts, Home Décor & Clothing

 C&T PUBLISHING

© Copyright 2002 Kathy MacMannis

Editor: Cyndy Lyle Rymer
Technical Editor: Sara Kate MacFarland
Copyeditor/Proofreader: Kerrie Smith
Cover Designer: Christina D. Jarumay
Design Director/Book Designer: Christina D. Jarumay
Illustrators: Kathy MacMannis Jeffery Carrillo
Production Assistant: Kirstie L. McCormick
Cutlet Wrangler: Lynn Koolish
Photography: Garry Gay, Amy Marson, Kirstie L. McCormick, Diane Pedersen
Published by C&T Publishing, Inc., P.O. Box 1456, Lafayette, California 94549

Front cover: American Flag Denim Jacket (see page 19) and Tea-Dyed
Flowerpot Rug (see page 20) by Kathy MacMannis. Photo by Garry Gay.
Many thanks to Margaret and Volney Peters for allowing us to photograph in
their home.
Back cover: Apple Peg Rack, Tissue Box and Vests; Rabbit Lap Throw; Sweet
Kids Angel; Dove Throw and Flower Wreath Pillow; Harvest Celebrations

Attention Teachers: C&T Publishing, Inc. encourages you to use this book as
a text for teaching. Contact us at 800-284-1114 or **www.ctpub.com** for
more information about the C&T Teachers Program.

Library of Congress Cataloging-in-Publication Data
MacMannis, Kathy,
  Rag wool appliqué : easy to sew-use any sewing machine-quilts, home
decor and clothing / Kathy MacMannis.
     p. cm.
  ISBN 1-57120-183-1
  1. Rugs, Hooked. 2. Appliqué. 3. Embroidery, Machine. I. Title.
  TT850 .M312 2002
  746--dc21
                              2002001350

Printed in China
10 9 8 7 6 5 4 3 2 1

Dedication

To my husband Russ, and three
children, Fraser, Laurie, and Tim.
Thank you for everything you've
had to endure, and for your
patience with the craziness that
often takes over our lives while
I try to fulfill my dreams.

CONTENTS

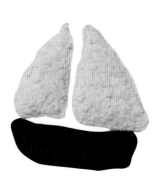

Introduction:
Roots of Rag Wool Appliqué

T raditional crafts and Americana have always been part of my life. One of my loves has been traditional rug hooking—creating small loops by pulling narrow strips of wool fabric through a burlap backing. Rug hooking has been around for hundreds of years. Our ancestors recycled old clothing and blankets to make rugs to add warmth to wood floors. These frugal women not only created rugs for warmth, they produced works of art for their floors. As with other folk art objects, these rugs have become cherished classics.

I hooked my first rug eight years ago. It measured 2' x 2½', and it took me hundreds of hours and almost four months to complete! Nothing can replace the beauty of a hand-hooked piece, but finding the time today to complete such a creation is simply impossible. This frustration about not having enough time to create another rug led me to develop my rag wool appliqué technique. With my knowledge of rug hooking, sewing, and machine-embroidery techniques, I was able to create the illusion of hand-worked pieces.

Several things contribute to the illusion. First, the fabric is 100 percent wool, which is cut into what I call *cutlets*. The cutlets are placed on a background, covered with a water-soluble stabilizer, and sewn down with invisible polyester thread. When the sewing is finished, the stabilizer is washed away, and water is absorbed by the cutlets, causing them to lift between the stitching lines. The result is a three-dimensional effect not unlike the loops in hand-hooked wool rugs. Creating the designs takes minutes rather than hours!

An added benefit is that the designs are appliqués, so you can use them to embellish not only fabric, but also ready-made items such as vests, jackets, lap throws, and even decorator items like wood tissue boxes.

I hope you enjoy *Rag Wool Appliqué*—and incorporate the techniques into your "sewing adventures!"

The projects are meant to inspire your creativity and provide multiple ways to use the rag wool appliqué designs. In developing the designs, I included a variety of applications and sewing techniques. Because we all have many demands on our time, I've used ready-made garments for the clothing projects, except for the Watercolor Floral Jacket on page 24. I hope you have fun with the technique and these designs.

Getting Started

Definitions

Throughout this book, I use terms that may be unfamiliar to you. Included below are definitions, along with an example of where the term is used.

Cutlets: Confetti-size pieces that are created by cutting narrow strips of wool into small ($1/4$" to $3/8$") squares. See page 8 to learn this process.

Cutlet Sandwich: After cutlets are arranged on a felt background, spray adhesive and stabilizer hold the cutlets in place, creating a "sandwich." See page 9 to learn this process.

Hooping: The term used for the process of inserting the cutlet sandwich into an embroidery hoop. See page 10 to learn this process.

Lip: Felt pieces are joined by creating a "lip" or "shelf." See page 14 to learn this process.

Supplies, Tools, and Fabrics

Stocking your supply closet and equipping your work area for rag wool appliqué is easy. You may already have many of the tools and fabrics that you will need. Below is a list of the basics. Following the list are more details about the various items.

Some project-specific supplies and tools are required. Be sure to read the supply list before beginning a project.

SUPPLIES

Water-soluble stabilizer, medium to heavy-weight (see Resources on page 63)
Temporary spray adhesive, such as Sulky KK2000®
Small, clear plastic bags
Permanent markers, extra-fine and medium tip
Water-soluble marking pens or pencils
Chalk pencils, Double-stick tape

Cutting Tools

Rotary cutting supplies: gridded mat, 6" x 24" acrylic ruler, and rotary cutter, scissors

Sewing tools

Sewing machine or computerized embroidery machine
Darning, open-toe appliqué, or embroidery presser foot
Dual-feed or "walking foot" (optional)
Jeans/Denim sewing machine needles, sizes 90 or 100
Invisible polyester (not nylon) thread in clear and smoke; I recommend Sulky® (see Resources on page 63)
All-purpose thread
Embroidery hoop(s), 6", 8", and 10" sizes (optional for conventional machines)
Hand-sewing needles
Straight pins, $3/4$" to 1"
Seam gauge or ruler
Steam iron

TIP: *You Can Use ANY Sewing OR Embroidery Machine to create these appliqué designs. It isn't even necessary that the machine have zigzag capabilities. An embroidery machine makes the work a little easier, but is not essential.* **The important thing to remember is that you should use the design as provided.** **DO NOT** *alter the size. See page 10 for more information.*

TIP: *The CD-ROM contains the design files in the various embroidery machine formats. You will need conversion software to utilize the CD-ROM.*
There is a folder for each group of projects with a separate folder for each machine format. Some designs, such as the rabbit in the Leaping Rabbit projects (page 44), are larger than 4", so some machines require that the design be sewn in separate segments. The segmented designs require separate hoopings. The folder containing the rabbit projects is divided as follows: Rabbit (the entire rabbit), RabbitP1, RabbitP2, RabbitP3 (P represents "Part"). Also included in the project folder is an Adobe Acrobat file showing how to put the parts together, and any additional notes.

FABRICS

100% wool in a variety of colors and patterns
Acrylic craft felt

Some projects use additional fabrics, such as lining fabric for a jacket, or fabric for a throw or pillow.

Selecting and Preparing Wool

The beauty of rag wool appliqué, aside from its appearance, is that you can transform scraps and otherwise useless pieces of wool into exciting designs. It is important, however, that you select wool that will compact or *felt* nicely when prewashed and becomes soft and fluffy when dried.

One hundred percent wools are ideal. Wool containing 7 to 10 percent nylon is also acceptable and will create the same effect. Most tweeds contain nylon fibers and will work for the rag wool technique as well.

Start with small quantities of wool. After you have played with the technique, expand your stash of wool, experimenting with solid colors, stripes, plaids, checks, and tweeds.

You may wish to use recycled wool. Clothing is a good source of fabric at less cost than new yardage. Raid your closet, or scour thrift shops. Look for wool with a tight weave. Sort by color and prewash wool. Avoid wool that is loosely woven even after drying in a hot dryer, and blends that boast that they are machine washable and dryable. Neither works well for rag wool appliqué. Washing and drying is a good way to test a mystery fabric, too. If it does not tighten up after being in the hot dryer, chances are it may have a high nylon content, and you should avoid using it.

To ensure that you are working with insect-free fabric that is 100 percent wool, prewash clothing with detergent in hot water and dry it in a hot dryer. Garments should come out of the dryer feeling soft and should have shrunk, to the point where they might fit a three-year-old. Your wool is now felted.

If you use new wool for appliqués, prewashing is unnecessary unless noted in the project instructions.

TIP: *Throughout these instructions, I often suggest one or more 9" x 14" pieces of wool for cutting into cutlets. Store unused cutlets in plastic bags for use in other rag wool appliqués. I store colors separately in individual bags. The pieces stay clean and organized, and the colors are easy to spot when I am creating appliqués.*

When creating a design, I try to include several different shades or accent colors. This results in a more interesting effect, and adds to the character of the design. It is fun to combine different shades of wool to create your favorite mixes. Hand-dyed wools are an option because they often contain a full spectrum of shades or tones of a single color. When you use hand-dyed wool in your appliqués, you create instant shading with gorgeous results. (See Resources on page 63 for sources for 100 percent wool, hand-dyed wool, and prepackaged cutlets.)

TIP: *Tea Dying: Add an "aged look" to wool and appliqués by using a tea dye. For the tea bath, brew three tea bags in one cup of boiling water, and let the bags steep for five minutes.*

Apply the tea to the fabric with a sponge brush, painting some areas more heavily than others. To create a darker stained area, place a tea bag directly on top of the piece for several minutes. As you work, remember that the fabric may be a lighter color when it dries than it appears when it is wet. It is better to apply the tea sparingly at first, because you can always apply more if you prefer a darker look.

Acrylic Felt

For best results, use 100 percent acrylic craft felt for the base of the appliqué designs.

As a base fabric, felt has several advantages over other fabrics. It is nonwoven, so cut edges will not fray, and you can cut along the bias without worrying about stretching and distortion. Felt is inexpensive and available in many colors, so you can coordinate it with the wool you are using for the design. Buy the colors you need in one-yard increments so you always have a selection on hand. There are differences in the weights of felt, however, so try to use those made by the same manufacturer for each project.

Yardage amounts for felt are not included in the instructions because you can stitch several appliqués on a single base.

Everything You Need to Know About the Supplies and Tools

THREADS

Upper thread: Anchoring the wool cutlets with invisible polyester thread helps create the illusion of rug hooking. This thread is available in two colors: clear and smoke. For lighter fabrics, use clear; darker fabrics require smoke. You might not think this is such a big deal, but the wrong color on the wool really does stand out. I have mistakenly or lazily used the wrong color only to consign the designs to the box of "goofs" that I bring to my classes to show students what not to do.

I only use Sulky™ invisible *polyester* thread because it tolerates a hot iron and does not melt, as other brands made of nylon do.

Bobbin thread: Use all-purpose sewing thread in a contrasting color for the bobbin. Using a contrasting thread allows you to check the tension easily because the thread can be seen against the background. Also, the contrasting color makes the outline of the design easier to see when trimming the appliqués.

WATER-SOLUBLE STABILIZER

Using medium- to heavy-weight water-soluble stabilizer is critical to rag wool appliqué. The stabilizer covers the cutlets and holds them in place while you sew.

TIP: *Always begin each project with stabilizer that has been stored properly.*

The biggest problem with most water-soluble stabilizers is they tend to dry out when they are exposed to air for extended periods, which causes them to split or tear. For best results, always store stabilizer in a sealed plastic bag.

If your stabilizer splits while you are stitching an applique, stop sewing immediately and apply a fresh layer of stabilizer that is at least 1¹/₂" larger, all around the split.

TIP: *Do not, under any circumstance, wet the stabilizer in an attempt to mend the split or tear.*

TEMPORARY ADHESIVE SPRAY

I recommend temporary adhesive spray to control the placement of the cutlets during construction; the spray also helps reduce the likelihood of air pockets developing in the appliqués. I use Sulky KK2000 temporary adhesive spray because it is nontoxic and won't gum up the needle. (See Resources on page 63.)

NEEDLES

Use Jeans/Denim sewing machine needles in sizes 90 or 100. They have a strong shaft and do not bend as easily as other needles. Using this type of needle, and sewing at a slower speed, greatly reduces the frequency of needle breaks. If your needles continue to break, reassess the thickness of the cutlet sandwich. Sewing with sharp needles makes the process easier. I strongly recommend that you change needles after every eight hours of sewing.

HOOPS FOR CONVENTIONAL SEWING MACHINES

Hoops are not necessary for rag wool appliqué, but do help to keep the layers of the cutlet sandwich together. To accommodate the height of the presser foot, hoops should have narrow rims, or a notched area that will make it easier to maneuver the hoop under the presser foot. Hoops are inexpensive and available in various sizes from fabric and craft stores, or through mail-order companies (see Resources on page 63). For the projects in this book, I recommend 6", 8", and 10" hoops. Choose a hoop at least 1¹/₂" to 2" larger all around than the appliqué design.

HOOPS FOR EMBROIDERY MACHINES

Hoops come in a variety of shapes and sizes, and are used to keep the layers of the cutlet sandwich taut while your machine sews out a design. Consult your machine's operating manual to set the hoop size on your machine.

General Instructions

Please take the time to read through **all** of the following steps before you begin a project. The same instructions apply to each project. The only difference in each project is how you apply the appliqué. Do not cut out the appliqué or trim any of the cutlet edges until you read through the project instructions.

For practice and to help get you started, step-by-step instructions for making a heart appliqué follow.

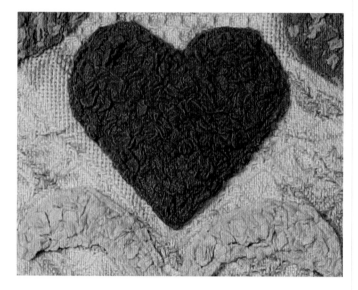

Creating the Appliqués

CUTTING THE WOOL

Throughout the book I refer to rotary cutting tools. Knowing how to precisely measure and cut using these tools is a fantastic timesaver and will give you wonderful results.

1. Using your rotary cutting tools, cut strips that are $1/4$" to $3/8$" wide from wool fabric. You do not need to measure precisely; you can simply eyeball the approximate width while cutting the strips. Varying the width of the strips is fine.

2. Turn the narrow strips of wool 90° and cut them again, creating confetti-size pieces $1/4$" to $3/8$" square. You have just created hundreds of little pieces of wool, or *cutlets*.

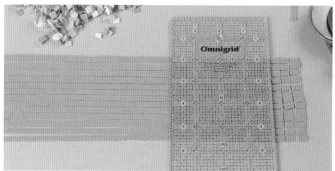

Cut the strips across to create *cutlets*.

3. Separate the cutlets by color, and store in plastic bags until you are ready to use them.

Preparing for Sewing

Those of you with embroidery machines will love the convenience of using the stitching designs provided on the CD. You won't need to trace the design onto the stabilizer.

TIP: *The design templates on pages 51-62 are provided for those of you who will use a conventional sewing machine. You will be able to sew with a straight stitch. The templates have heavy dots to indicate where sewing begins, and arrows that indicate the sewing direction for each piece. The dots are located just below the entrance to the interior of each shape, where the stippling stitches that are used to anchor the cutlets begin, to create a slight overlap in the outline prior to sewing the inner stitches.*

Experiment with and without a hoop to see what works best for you. If you choose to use a hoop, select one that is at least $1 1/2$" to 2" larger all around than the appliqué design. For example, use a 6" hoop for the heart design. If you don't use a hoop, you will need to use more spray adhesive to anchor the cutlets.

1. Cut the stabilizer at least 4" larger all around than the design. Lightly spray one side of the stabilizer with temporary adhesive.

2. Center the stabilizer, sticky side down, over the design template (the heart pattern is on page 58). Use a medium-tip permanent marker to trace the outline and all inner stitching lines of the design onto the stabilizer.

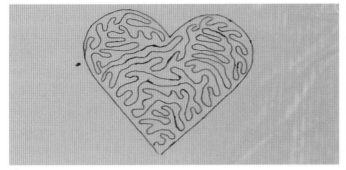

Trace outline and inner stitching lines onto stabilizer.

TIP: *For darker wool it may help to use a double layer of stabilizer so you can see the stitching lines. Experiment. If you use two layers of stabilizer be sure to wash it all out when you are finished creating the appliqué.*

Use a marker in a contrasting color to trace the pattern onto the stabilizer. Otherwise, you may have a difficult time following the lines.

Making the Cutlet Sandwich

Cutting and preparing the felt base: Cut a coordinating piece of felt for the base of the design. It should be at least 2" larger all around than the hoop measurement, or 4" larger than the design area if a hoop is not used. For the heart, cut an 8" square of blue felt. Use a marker or chalk pencil to draw a light outline of the design on the foundation felt as a guide for placing the cutlets. Lightly spray the felt base with temporary adhesive to hold the cutlets in place.

Trace the outline on the felt.

Placing the cutlets: Place some cutlets in the center of the felt. Continue adding to the cutlet pile until the cutlets extend at least 1" beyond the outline of the design. Work from the center toward the edge to prevent air pockets. (Use the pattern traced on the stabilizer as a guide; hold the stabilizer over the pile every so often to see how many more cutlets you need to add.)

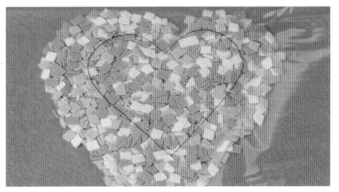

Place the cutlets so they extend 1" beyond the outline. (Inner stippling stitches not shown.)

Height of the cutlet pile: Use the palm of your hand to firmly compress the cutlets until the pile is approximately $1/4$"–$3/8$" thick and extends 1" beyond all edges of the design. If you plan to use a hoop, avoid piling cutlets higher than the rim of the hoop. For best results, maintain the same thickness throughout the cutlet pile, all the way to the edge of the design.

Compress the pile of cutlets to about $1/4$".

Color accents: To create different effects, simply sprinkle a few cutlets in an accent color(s) over the pile. Off-white cutlets were generously added to blue cutlets for the heart. I sprinkled some gold cutlets in the flag on the cover's denim jacket to add a little sparkle. On the apple design (page 52), different shades of red or a contrasting color such as green add nice accents. For a tweed effect, toss or mix together cutlets in several colors. I have developed formulas that I use consistently because I like the effect. For example, one of my favorite formulas for black begins with four parts black (one part equals one $1/4$"-wide wool strip). I add one part each of dark hunter green and dark burgundy. Experiment to develop formulas that you like.

Pressing the cutlet pile: Steam-press (do not drag the iron across) the cutlet pile. Pressing condenses the pile and reduces air pockets, making it easier to sew. Avoid getting the wool too wet. Use a medium iron setting so the heat won't melt the acrylic felt. Check the pile as you work to make sure you don't see gaps, or exposed areas of the felt base between the cutlets (to fix gaps, see page 13). Let the wool cool before applying the layer of stabilizer.

Using a hoop: Place the top (smaller) hoop temporarily over the cutlet pile. Remove any cutlets that are under the rim of the hoop. Remove the top hoop.

Lightly spray temporary adhesive over the cutlets and edges of the felt, and center the stabilizer (with the traced pattern) sticky side down on top of the wool cutlets. Firmly press the stabilizer to the cutlets and surrounding area. Keep the stabilizer taut, without wrinkles. You have now created a "cutlet sandwich."

Place the top (smaller) hoop over the cutlet sandwich (felt on the bottom, cutlet filling with stabilizer on top). Grasp the felt, stabilizer, and top hoop and insert the sandwich into the bottom (larger) hoop. Gently pull the edges of the felt, making the fabric taut within the hoop. You are now ready to stitch your cutlet sandwich. The next step is to prepare your sewing machine.

Place the hoop over the cutlet sandwich and pull felt taut. (Stippling stitches not shown.)

Setting Up Your Machine

Before you start sewing, clean your machine. This applies to both conventional sewing machines and embroidery machines. While stitching wool and felt, "fuzzies" build up around the needle and bobbin, which can create real problems. I suggest that you clean the bobbin area each time you insert a newly wound bobbin. Be kind to your machine and it will work like a charm.

TENSION CHECKS FOR ALL MACHINES

Because the appliqué is much thicker than fabric, you may need to adjust the presser foot tension and stitch length. Refer to your machine's operating manual. You may also need to adjust the upper thread tension when you use invisible polyester thread. See page 11 for directions to check the upper thread tension.

Setting Up All Embroidery Machines

In the last several years sewing machine manufacturers have developed wonderful embroidery machines for home use, allowing creative freedom that had previously been reserved for commercial use. Using the CD-Rom provided, the embroidery machine does the stitching for you. You simply choose the design and hoop the cutlets. The only limitation is the size of the embroidery machine's sewing field. Older machines tend to have a 4" square sewing field, while newer machines accommodate hoops up to 6"-9". Where possible, I've tried to keep the design elements to 4".

TIP: *Do not alter the size of the design in your software or on your machine. Doing so changes the space between the stitches and the cutlets will either fall out or be compressed too much.*

Certain designs, such as the rabbit, are larger than 4", and are made in segments that need to be pieced unless you own a machine that is capable of sewing this size design. Piecing instructions begin on page 14.

1. Follow the General Instructions for cutting and preparing the cutlets for stitching. Center the design in the hoop and be sure the cutlet pile extends 1" beyond all areas to be sewn. No cutlets should be under the hoop itself.

2. Set up your embroidery machine as though you were going to embroider through quilted fabric. Depending on your machine, this may require adjusting the presser foot tension and/or using a specific foot, as outlined below in Step 3. Refer to your machine's operating manual. Most newer machines have self-adjusting features and do not require as many manual adjustments.

3. Use a Jeans/Denim needle, invisible polyester thread, and a bobbin wound with contrasting thread. Use clear invisible polyester thread for lighter wools, and smoke-colored invisible polyester thread for darker colors. Transfer the desired design file to your embroidery machine.

4. Adjust the upper tension as needed until the stitch is balanced, that is, until there are no dots of bobbin thread visible on top of the appliqué sandwich. There is no need to adjust the stitch length. Record your adjustments for future reference.

5. Follow the remaining General Instructions to create the design. Practice using the heart design (page 59).

TIP: *Don't leave for a cup of tea just yet. Stay near your machine while it is stitching. You need to be there in case the stabilizer splits.*

Setting Up All Conventional Sewing Machines

As mentioned previously, you may sew with or without a hoop. Try both methods on a test piece to see which works best for you. Also, practice the technique with the feed dogs in both the "up" and "down" positions.

Practice using the heart design (page 59). After you have prepared the cutlet sandwich, sew one or two inches of the outline before adjusting the stitch length and upper thread tension. Note the adjustments you make so you can quickly set your machine the next time you sew rag wool appliqués.

1. Follow the General Instructions for cutting and preparing the cutlets. Center the design in the hoop and be sure the cutlet pile extends 1" beyond all areas to be sewn. Cutlets should not be under the hoop.

2. Use a Jeans/Denim needle, invisible polyester thread, and a bobbin wound with all-purpose thread in a con-

trasting color. Use clear invisible polyester thread for lighter wools and smoke for darker ones. Avoid using the wrong color invisible polyester thread; it makes a big difference and will be as noticeable as a sore thumb! Select a bobbin thread color that contrasts slightly with the felt base, so you can see the outline of the design when you cut out the appliqué.

3. Select a presser foot. The easiest to use are a darning foot, an open-toe appliqué foot, or an embroidery foot. I also had success using a dual-feed, or "walking foot." If you use this foot, you may need a larger hoop to accommodate the clearance for turning the design.

4. You may also need to adjust the presser foot pressure or tension on your machine. Refer to your machine's operating manual. Most machines have a spring-loaded control or wheel that controls the pressure, or an intermediate position for the presser foot.

Strive for a pressure that allows you to move the hoop freely, so the presser foot won't dig into the cutlet sandwich. If you have fully released the tension of the presser foot and it continues to dig into the sandwich, hindering movement, check and adjust the depth of the cutlet pile as necessary. The pile should be no thicker than $1/4$" after you compress it with a steam iron.

TIP: *Note that it is also possible to leave the presser foot tension as is, and drop the feed dogs instead, as you would for free-motion stitching. The stitch length does not have to be consistent; the stitches do need to be close together.*

5. Find the proper stitch length first (9-12 stitches per inch), then adjust the upper tension; record the settings for both. Refer to the stitching pattern and begin sewing the design outline at the dot, backstitching several times. Sew one or two inches, and remove the piece from the machine.

TIP: *Always sew design outlines first.*

6. Turn the piece over so the back (felt) side is up. Using a seam gauge or ruler, count the number of stitches per inch. Again, there should be 9–12 stitches per inch.

7. Starting where you left off, reposition the piece beneath the needle, adjust the stitch length if necessary, and sew another inch. Check the back again for stitch length. Record the proper stitch length for future reference.

TIP: *If your machine has the needle-down feature, use it while sewing. When making turns, leave the needle down, and lift the presser foot when turning the sandwich.*

8. Remove the piece again and recheck the top of the appliqué sandwich. If you see small "dots" of bobbin thread, loosen the upper tension (if you have not loosened it already), reposition the piece beneath the needle, and sew another inch.

TIP: *Check and adjust the tension until the dots of bobbin thread are gone. Achieving a balanced stitch will most likely require a tension adjustment due to the strength of the invisible polyester thread.*

Once you have made the adjustments, record the upper tension setting, then finish sewing the outline.

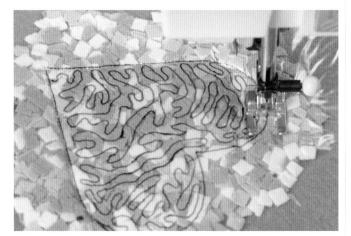

Sew the outline first.

9. Sew the inner stippling stitches, adjusting the presser-foot pressure as needed. It's important to follow the marked sewing lines on the stabilizer. A stitch that strays from the sewing lines here or there won't make much difference, but if your stitches vary too much, you run the risk of creating areas where the space between the lines is too great, causing the cutlets to fall out. As you sew, look slightly ahead of the needle. With practice, you will be able to move the piece without even thinking about it.

10. After you finish the inner stitching, backstitch several times to secure the invisible polyester thread.

11. For designs that require piecing, see Piecing Together Design Segments on page 14.

Finishing the Appliqué

TRIMMING THREADS AND REMOVING THE STABILIZER

When you have finished sewing the design, remove it from the machine and trim all threads. Scoop up leftover cutlets and return them to their plastic bags for use in other appliqués.

TIP: *Do not trim the cutlet edges or cut out the appliqué until you have read individual project instructions. If you wish, you may trim the excess felt away, but be sure to leave a 2" border of felt at this time.*

Trimming extra stabilizer: If you used a hoop, remove it. Trim the excess stabilizer from the edges of the design. Avoid tearing away the stabilizer, which can pull stitches.

Carefully trim the excess stabilizer.

TIP: *You will notice that there are cutlets of various lengths extending from the sewn border. Leave this edge ragged for now; many projects require that one or more edges remain untrimmed.*

Leave the ragged edges untrimmed.

Removing the stabilizer: To remove the stabilizer, place the appliqué under running water. As the stabilizer dissolves, work the design using your fingers—rake your fingers back and forth over the design to help lift the fibers. To felt properly, the wool needs to be thoroughly saturated with water. As you work, you will see the cutlet layers puff up like magic before your eyes!

Drying: Wring the appliqué, squeezing out as much water as possible. Then, tumble dry for about 20 minutes. If time isn't an issue, air-drying works too. Don't over-dry the wool. It will be fine if it is somewhat damp.

TIP: *A word of caution: Avoid drying different colors of wool together in the dryer, even if you feel the colors are "close enough." The renegade fuzz will jump to other areas of the design. Wait until you have completed all the pieces in the same color (all the reds, for example) before drying the wool.*

Fixing Gaps in the Design

1. Once the design is dry, inspect it for gaps or areas where the background felt peeks through. Gaps along the outline are easy to fix as you sew the appliqué to the item you are embellishing. When you come to a bare spot, stop sewing, lift the presser foot, place a cutlet or two, lower the presser foot, and continue sewing.

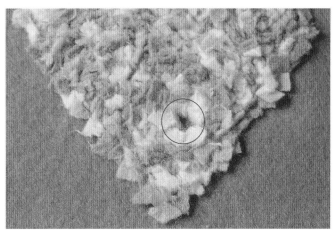

Gaps in the design can easily be fixed.

2. Fix other gaps in the pile by hand. Choose a $^3/_8$"–$^1/_2$" long cutlet. Thread a hand-sewing needle using thread to match the color of the cutlet; double the thread and tie a knot. From the back of the felt, bring the needle through to the front. Thread the cutlet through its center onto the needle. Take a small stitch back through the cutlet's center and through to the back of the felt. Pull the thread snugly, working the cutlet into the bare spot. (The cutlet will fold onto itself, making a V shape.) Repeat with additional cutlets until the bare spot is adequately covered.

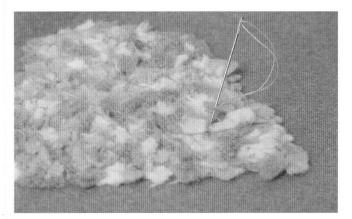

Thread a cutlet onto a needle to fix gaps.

3. From the front, trim the added piece or pieces of wool so they are the same height as the rest of the design.

4. If necessary, steam-press the finished design. If you are using Sulky invisible polyester thread, press the top of the design, or press from the back of the felt.

Trimming the Edges of the Appliqué

Individual project instructions contain information about cutting out the appliqués, piecing them together when necessary, trimming the seam allowances to the appropriate width, and so on.

TIP: *Be sure to read through the project instructions* **completely** *before trimming the cutlets and cutting out your rag wool design.*

Trimming: When the directions call for the appliqué to be trimmed, use sharp scissors to trim the ragged cutlet edges so none are longer than $1/4$", refining the shape.

Cutting out the designs: When you cut out the appliqué, work from the back of the design, using the contrasting bobbin-thread outline as a guide. Unless the directions state otherwise, trim the felt edge of the appliqué $1/8$" outside the outline stitches. Avoid cutting any of the invisible polyester threads. After trimming, the background felt should not be visible when looking at the appliqué from the top.

Seam allowance for design segments that require piecing: Leave $1/2$" of felt around all edges.

Applying the Appliqués

For some projects, you can simply glue or tack rag wool appliqués in position. Sewing them in place, however, sometimes requires a few more steps.

PIECING TOGETHER DESIGN SEGMENTS

Some of the larger designs, such as the rabbit, may need to be created in segments. The segments are then pieced together to create the complete design. Follow this simple technique for a join that is nearly invisible. Use a Jeans/Denim needle.

1. Create all the design segments. Cut away the excess stabilizer, and brush away extra cutlets. Rinse and dry all pieces. Leave all edges of the design ragged at this point. Follow the instructions and illustrations below to trim and join the pieces into one unit.

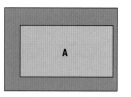 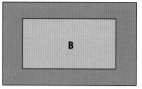

Trim the edge to be joined close to the stitching line.   **Leave $1/2$"-wide seam allowance around all edges.**

2. Begin by creating a "lip" or "shelf" on piece B. Using the contrasting bobbin thread as a guide, trim excess felt from each side of piece B, leaving a $1/2$"-wide seam allowance all around.

3. For piece A, trim the felt close to the stitching line, along the edge that will connect with piece B. Remove the felt only along the edge that will connect to piece B. Leave excess felt on the remaining sides of piece A.

4. Place a strip of double-stick tape on the back of A, along the trimmed edge that will be joined to piece B. Place the edge of piece A on top of the lip you created on piece B. Press the two edges together, squishing them so the ragged cutlets along the edge blend together. Flip the section over to check the placement; the outlines should look continuous and the join should be invisible. From the right side, using invisible polyester thread, sew piece A to piece B (sewing over the previous outline stitching on piece A.) Open the seam and remove the tape.

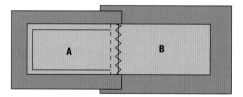

Place piece A on top of piece B and stitch along the outline stitching. See tip on page 15 for using zigzag stitch.

SEWING THE APPLIQUÉS IN PLACE

1. Prior to pinning and stitching in place, lightly spray the back of the design using temporary spray adhesive to minimize shifting while you sew the appliqué.

2. The easiest way to sew rag wool appliqués in place is simply to sew over the previously stitched outline using invisible polyester thread and straight stitches. Use a Jeans/Denim needle and maintain the same upper tension that you used for stitching down the cutlets.

Use a walking foot if you have one; those feed dogs can be a big help! Or, if your machine has limited presser-foot lift, use a blind hemstitch or blanket stitch, just catching the edge of the appliqué on the background.

TIP: *If you are applying designs that have pieced segments, and are making a wallhanging, picture, table rug, or anything that does not have to be flexible, you can stop at the end of step 2.*

TIP: *For garments that are intended to be supple, I add a step 3: Using narrow zigzag stitches, sew along the seam between pieces A and B using invisible polyester thread. This prevents the appliqué from folding back and exposing the joined area.*

Sewing Tips

BORDERS

It may be necessary to piece border strips for the length needed. Unless otherwise stated, piece together borders on the diagonal to create a smooth seam. Place the two strips right sides together at a 90° angle, with a slight overlap. Stitch a diagonal seam as shown in the illustration. Trim the seam to $1/4$", press open, and trim the overlap.

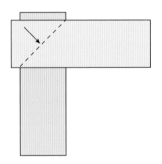

Stitch border lengths using diagonal seam.

PREVENTING "DOG EARS" ON PILLOWS

On better quality and custom-made pillows, corners appear perfectly square because all the outer edges of the fabric pieces were tapered prior to sewing. If you don't taper the edges you'll create "dog ears." The following technique prevents dog ears.

A 19" top (18" finished) is used as an example. Fold the fabric for the pillow top in half, then in quarters, to form a $9 1/2$" square. Using a wash-away marker, place a dot on each **unfolded edge** at the halfway mark ($4 3/4$").

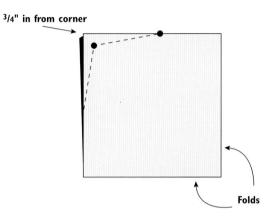

Place a dot on the unfolded edges.

From the unfolded corner, measure $3/4$" in on the diagonal, and mark the spot with a dot. Use a ruler to draw a line from the side dots to the corner dot. Trim the fabric along these lines and open the top.

You've just created equally tapered edges!

Fold the top and bottom of lightweight fabrics at the same time. But for heavier fabrics and projects that require battings and backings, taper each corner separately. In this case, taper the top and then use it as a pattern for the remaining corners.

One of the exciting things about rag wool appliqué is that it is so versatile: you can add the appliqués to just about anything! These apple projects are designed to be quick and easy, help you learn this lively craft, and suggest ways you can use rag wool designs. For example, you can appliqué them onto a ready-made item as shown, or create a wooden tissue box and peg rack, "aging" them with paint before applying the apples.

Apple Tea Towel and Vest

For a quick gift, add a rag wool apple to a purchased towel or vest and…Presto!

SUPPLIES AND TOOLS

One 8" square red wool for each apple
One 6" square dark green wool for each apple's leaves
Scrap of brown wool or jute twine for each apple stem
Dark red and green felt for the base of each appliqué
Purchased tea towel or fleece vest
Additional supplies and tools noted in Getting Started
(page 5)

INSTRUCTIONS

1. Use the apple and leaf patterns (page 52) and follow the General Instructions (page 8) to create the apple and leaf appliqués.
You may create multiple leaves at one time; just remember to allow at least 1" between each leaf design.
2. Create as many leaves as desired.
3. Pin one apple, two leaves, and a stem to the tea towel or vest, tucking the stem under the leaf.
4. Stitch the appliqués to the tea towel or vest following the General Instructions (page 14).

Checkerboard Apple Tissue Box and Peg Rack

I antiqued this tissue box and peg rack using a simple process that I learned years ago. Don't they look like they have been sitting in someone's barn for a hundred years? I like the primitive country look. The secret to achieving this look is hide glue, a slow-binding adhesive found at many hardware stores. Substituting crackling medium will yield a similar finish. The paints are available at most craft stores. The variety of paint applications also contributes to the "aged look."

SUPPLIES AND TOOLS

One 6" square red wool for each apple (one for the tissue box ; three for the peg rack)
One 6" square dark green wool for each apple's leaves
Scrap of brown wool or of jute twine for each apple stem
Felt in coordinating colors for the base of each appliqué
Purchased, unfinished wooden tissue box
17" length of 1" x 8" pine, or plaque for peg rack
Three wood pegs for peg rack
Hide glue or crackling medium (I use Franklin's Hide Glue)
White and black acrylic craft paints
Light oil stain, such as golden oak
Dark oil stain, such as mahogany or walnut
Three 1"-wide beveled sponge brushes
Medium-grit sandpaper
Fine-tip paintbrush or black permanent marker, for details
Rag or paper towel
Craft glue, pencil, ruler

INSTRUCTIONS

1. Use the apple and leaf patterns (page 52) and follow the General Instructions (page 8) to create three apples and six leaves for the peg rack, or one apple and two leaves for the tissue box.
2. To create the checkerboard design, use a ruler and pencil to draw a 1"-wide border around the base of the tissue box and outer edge of the peg rack. Divide the border into 1" segments, fudging the width as necessary so you have an odd number of checks per side. Each side

of my tissue box measured 5¼", and I wanted to have five checks on each side. I made my checks bigger by a smidgen. For the 17" long peg rack, I marked seven checks. The width is actually less than 8". Remember that this is a primitive, simple design, so don't worry about precise measurements. "Eyeballing" the width is fine.

Diagrams for Apple Checkerboard Peg Rack and Tissue Box

TIP: *For safety's sake, take precautions when antiquing: Work in a well-ventilated area, preferably outside; wear latex gloves when handling stains; and wear safety glasses while sanding.*

1. Use a sponge brush to dab the hide glue randomly on the pine plaque and the wood pegs. The thicker you apply the glue, the larger the crackles will be, and the longer it will take to dry. Resist the urge to cover the entire surface with glue; nothing ages uniformly. An all-over application of glue will result in all-over crackling, diminishing the aged effect. Allow the glue to dry thoroughly, several hours or overnight.

2. On the tissue box, paint the area above the border white. Also apply white paint to the plaque's center rectangle and the three pegs. As soon as the paint touches the glued area, it will crackle. Do not repaint these sections. Allow to dry thoroughly.

3. Create the borders on the box and peg rack by applying white paint to every other block. On the plaque, paint a black square in each corner. Alternate white and black paint in the remaining blocks, and allow the paint to dry thoroughly.

4. Apply white paint to the narrow edges of the peg rack, and allow the paint to dry thoroughly.

5. Apply black paint to the remaining squares, and allow to dry thoroughly. Then, use a fine-tip paintbrush or indelible marker to paint or draw a thin black line above each white square. Allow to dry thoroughly.

6. Use medium-grit paper to sand all corners of the box or plaque. Distress the edges in random spots so the natural wood color shows through. Resist the urge to sand evenly. On my tissue box and peg rack, I sanded through to the bare wood in a few places.

7. Brush golden oak or honey-toned stain on all areas, including the sides, back, and pegs. Allow the stain to dry thoroughly.

8. Use a sponge brush or rag to dab areas of both projects with the dark mahogany or walnut stain. Allow the stain to dry for about 5 minutes, then blot the excess stain with a rag or paper towel. A bit of dark stain contributes to the aged and worn look. Allow to dry thoroughly.

9. Place the rag wool apple appliqués on the peg rack (refer to the photo). To determine placement for the peg holes, center the pegs under each apple. Drill a hole for each peg, add glue to the end of the peg, and insert it into the hole. Allow to dry thoroughly.

10. Using craft glue, attach the apples and leaves to the board or tissue box, tucking stems under leaves. I used a snip of jute twine for the stems.

American Flag Denim Jacket

Denim and Old Glory are pure Americana! Trim a jacket with this patriotic emblem, or make a simple wallhanging, framed piece, or appliqué it to a purse.

SUPPLIES AND TOOLS

6" square gold wool

One 9" x 14" rectangle navy wool

Three 9" x 14" rectangles dark red (burgundy) wool

Three 9" x 14" rectangles off-white wool

Felt in coordinating colors for the base of each appliqué

Navy cotton for the appliqué backing

Purchased denim jacket

Additional supplies and tools noted in Getting Started (page 5)

INSTRUCTIONS

1. Use the flag patterns (page 53) and follow the General Instructions (page 8) to create one gold star, one navy rectangle, five 5"-long red strips, and one 6"-long red strip. Also make three 5"-long off-white strips and two 6"-long off-white strips. Rinse like-color sections together and dry. Trim excess felt and ragged cutlets along the edges of the star. **Do not trim the felt or cutlets from any of the other pieces.**

2. Following the piecing technique in the General Instructions, piece and sew a red 5" strip to opposite sides of an off-white 5" strip, creating the "lips" on the white strip. After sewing, **do not trim any of the felt from the remaining edges.**

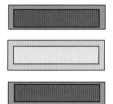

Sew each red strip to the center white strip. Leave edges ragged.

3. Piece and sew the navy rectangle to the end of the three stripes, creating the lip on the pieced stripes. After sewing, **do not trim felt from the remaining edges.**

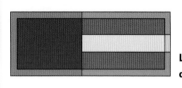

Sew the blue rectangle to the lip on the stripes.

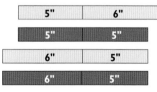

Leave $^1/_2$" of felt around all edges.

4. Piece together the red and off-white strips as shown below, joining them end-to-end. You will have longer strips than needed, but the extra length will allow you to offset the joins. It does not matter which side the lip is on. Do not remove any of the felt from the other sides.

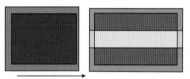

Piece and sew lengths end to end.

5. Piece together all of the flag elements, offsetting the seams as shown below.

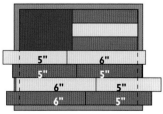

Leave $^1/_2$" of felt around all edges.

6. Trim the felt backing and extensions, leaving a ½"-wide seam allowance all around. Including the seam allowance, the flag should measure 8" x 10". Don't worry if the size is not exact because it adds to the charm of this folk art flag.

7. Cut the navy backing fabric so it matches the dimensions of your pieced flag. Layer the top and backing, right sides together, and stitch the front to the back in a ½"-wide seam. Sew on top of the previous outline stitches. Leave a 6" opening along the bottom edge. Clip the corners, and turn it right side out. Steam-press the flag. Slipstitch the opening closed.

8. Appliqué the flag to the jacket back using a straight or zigzag stitch around the edges. I also sew through some of the seams of the stripes to add greater stability.

Tea-Dyed Flowerpot Table Rug

Finished size: 14" x 23"

Flower designs are a favorite of mine because they can be used in such a variety of ways. Flowers come in all colors so choosing a theme is easy. I wanted the flowers to be bold and cheery, so I chose three green wools for the stems and leaves, dark brown for the pots, and an off-white woven fabric for the background. Then I decided the background was just too white for my décor, so I aged and softened it by tea dying (see page 6) after the project was complete.

SUPPLIES AND TOOLS

8" squares of wool in three colors for flowers
8" squares of wool in three greens for leaves and stems
Three 8" squares of dark brown wool for flowerpots
Felt in coordinating colors for the base of each appliqué
½ yard off-white woven cotton fabric for background
¾ yard black prewashed wool or black cotton for the backing and binding
15" x 24" cotton batting
Water-soluble marking pens or chalk pencils
Optional: Three tea bags and sponge paintbrush for tea dying
Additional supplies and tools noted in Getting Started (see page 5)

INSTRUCTIONS

1. Before you begin, cut and reserve a ½"-wide strip from each of the prewashed green wools for the flower stems. Also, if you have selected black wool yardage for backing and binding, before measuring it, prewash it in hot water and dry it in a hot dryer to shrink, soften and felt the wool.

2. Use the flowerpot patterns (pages 54-56) and follow the General Instructions (page 8) to create three brown flowerpots, one of each flower, and one of each set of leaves.

3. Create as many leaves as desired.

4. Cut away excess felt and ragged cutlets on flowerpots, flowers, and all edges of the leaves, **except the edges that abut the stems.** Leave the side of each leaf ragged along the stem edge.

5. From the felted black wool, cut two circles for flower centers; set them aside. Or, if you prefer, cut black wool into small cutlets and stitch on top of the black felt circles, making rag wool centers for two of the flowers. Set aside.

6. Cut the off-white cotton background fabric so it measures 14" x 23". Use a ruler and water-soluble marker or chalk pencil to draw a 1¼"-wide border around all edges.

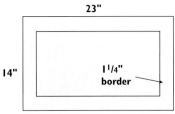

Draw a 1¼" border around all edges.

7. Lay the off-white background fabric over the cotton batting, and trim the batting even with the top. Spray a light coat of temporary adhesive over the batting to prevent shifting. Make sure there are no wrinkles in the fabric or batting.

8. Square up the edges of the felted black wool, and smooth it out on a tabletop, wrong side up. Center the batting and top over the black wool, allowing at least $2\frac{1}{2}$" around all edges. When it is positioned correctly, fold back half of the batting and lightly spray it with temporary adhesive. Smooth the batting, and repeat for the other half. Use rotary cutting tools to trim the backing so there is 2" around all edges.

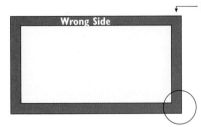

— 2"

Wrong Side

Trim the backing larger than the batting all around. (The circle indicates the details in the next two illustrations.)

9. The following technique eliminates bulkiness in the corners. Practice on a 6" square scrap of cotton fabric first, so you can clearly see the lines you will press into the corners. Mark a 2"-deep border along two adjoining sides of the scrap. Fold one 2"-wide border strip in half lengthwise and press. Fold the strip in half again, up to the top; press. Unfold. Repeat for the adjoining side. When you open the pressed edges, notice that the intersecting lines in the corner create four squares.

Folds create four squares.

10. Remove these squares, but maintain at least a $\frac{1}{4}$"–$\frac{1}{2}$" area from the inner edge for turning under. Wool and heavy fabrics, such as fleece, require a $\frac{1}{2}$" allowance. Cut the corner of your practice piece as shown in the illustration that follows, leaving the turn-under allowance intact along one side. Then, fold, press, open, and cut each of the corners for the table rug.

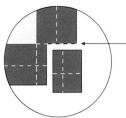

At the arrow, cut the binding away along the fold line. Leave $\frac{1}{4}$"–$\frac{1}{2}$" for turn-under allowance.

11. To finish each corner, start with the right-hand edge, and refold the backing twice. Pin it to the top. Refold the bottom edge twice, and pin. Repeat on remaining three corners. The raw edges of the binding should not be visible. What should be visible is $\frac{1}{4}$" of the border initially marked on the off-white background (in step 6). Fold and pin all four corners. Edge-stitch the binding to the top along the fold line.

12. To prepare the appliqués, use invisible polyester thread to stitch the black wool flower centers (from step 5) to the blue and yellow flowers.

13. Use the photo as a guide and arrange the pots, flowers, and leaves inside the marked border. Place the stems first, then the leaves. Tuck the ends of the stems under the flower and pot. When you are pleased with the placement, pin the pieces in place and use invisible polyester thread to machine stitch them to the background. For the stems, stitch down the center of each strip. Optional: Echo quilt around each flower and pot. Optional: Tea dye the background.

TIP: *To achieve an aged look, or to tone down a bright white or color, tea dye the fabric. See page 6 for tea dying instructions.*

SUPPLIES AND TOOLS

8" square light blue wool

Two 8" squares pale pink wool

Felt in coordinating colors for the base of each appliqué

Ready-made jacket or vest

Additional supplies and tools noted in Getting Started (page 5)

INSTRUCTIONS

1. Use the patterns (page 57) and follow the General Instructions (page 8) to create one 4" blue square and the four pink quarter triangles.

TIP: *It is very important that you sew the outline edges of the design accurately so your pieces will properly align. It is especially important that the color of the bobbin thread sharply contrasts with the color of the felt base.*

2. For all edges of the square, and the 4" (long) edges of the triangles, stitch an additional line ¹/₈"–¹/₄" inside the outline.

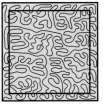

Sew a line ¹/₈" to ¹/₄" inside the outline.

This extra line will provide support after the seams are sewn and pressed open.

 tone-washed cotton denim is one of my favorite fabrics, and complements the hand-dyed wools used in this project.

Blue Suede Jacket with Quilt Block Design

This powder blue suede jacket is rich in color and texture and I thought it would be perfect for a simple patchwork design. This project features an alternative method for piecing the design elements similar to quilt piecing, but with a few variations. It takes a little patience, and precise cutting and sewing, but you'll create perfect points. The project is small enough to prevent frustration!

TIP: *Be sure all cutlet edges are left ragged, and that there is at least 1" of felt along all edges.*

3. Rinse and dry the pieces. If the pieces curl, press them flat with a steam iron. Gently tug on the shape to ensure that the edges are 4" square.

4. Lay the 4" square face down on the cutting mat. Place your clear acrylic ruler over the felt and align the outside stitching line with the 1/2" line on the ruler.

5. You should be able to see the contrasting bobbin thread through the clear ruler. Using a rotary cutter, trim away the excess felt so you create a 1/2"-wide seam allowance. Repeat on all sides of the square. Your felt square should now measure 5". Repeat the process for each of the triangles. When you are finished, all pieces should have a 1/2"-wide seam allowance.

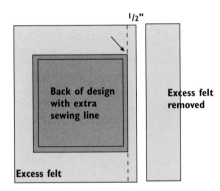

Line up the outline with the 1/2" mark on the ruler.

6. With right sides together, and matching the edges, place the 4" side of one triangle on top of one of the 4" sides of the square. The edges of the triangle will extend beyond the edges of the square, but the stitching lines should match up perfectly. If one of the sides is a little off, stretch it gently until the stitching lines match.

7. Insert pins parallel to the edge within the seam allowance.

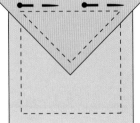

Place pins in the 1/2"-wide seam allowance.

Use a Jeans/Denim needle and thread that complements the wool color to machine-baste (a longer stitch length) the two sections together. You will sew directly over the outline stitches.

8. Open the seam and check the stitching. When the seams align perfectly, reset the stitch length and sew again. Press the seams open. Repeat the process for the opposite side. Press open. Repeat for the remaining two triangles.

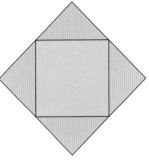

The finished block

The completed design should look like a square-within-a-square, as shown.

9. Trim the remaining felt from the outer edges of the design, close to the stitching line, and clean up the ragged cutlet edges.

10. Use invisible polyester thread to sew the design to the back of the garment.

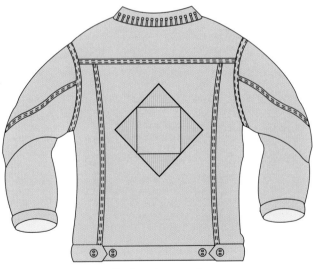

Design placement

Watercolor Floral Jacket

The inspiration for this jacket came from my collection of hand-dyed wool. The colors reminded me of a watercolor painting. I had coordinating pastel homespuns in my fabric stash, so I chose to make the jacket. The pattern is "Everyday Jackets" from Taylor Made Designs (see Resources on page 63). When selecting a pattern I chose a loose fitting, mid-length design and added the 3" homespun strip at the bottom, creating a base for the vase to sit on, and also coordinated with the cuffs. There is no right or wrong way to construct your floral arrangement. For this project you are given the basic guidelines and necessary elements, but you are the florist!

> **TIP:** *If you plan to make the matching purse on page 25, purchase enough fabric for both the jacket and purse.*

SUPPLIES AND TOOLS

8" square each pink, yellow, and blue wool

Three to four different shades of green wool for leaves and stems (Each flower has a slightly different set of leaf colors.)

One piece prewashed green wool at least 14" x 3" long for the stems and additional leaves

9" x 14" rectangle muted brown wool for vase

Felt in coordinating colors for the base of each appliqué

Ready-made jacket or vest

Additional supplies and tools noted in Getting Started (page 5)

INSTRUCTIONS

1. Prepare the wool as directed in the General Instructions (page 8), but DO NOT cut up the long piece of green that is to be used for the stems and additional leaves. Be sure to keep the cutlets separated!

2. Use the tulip, vase and large leaf patterns (pages 54–56) and follow the General Instructions (page 8) to create the tulip, vase, and large leaf.

Design variation for remaining two flowers: Notice that the two flowers have the centers incorporated into the design. For this project I wanted a subtle effect, and felt that this treatment achieved that. Create the mound of cutlets as described, and steam-press the pile. Remove a small pinch of cutlets from the center, no larger than a nickel. Place the contrasting color cutlets in the the center and steam-press again. For the blue flower I used brown for center, and pink for the yellow flower. Keep in mind that the pile compacts down even more when sewn, which creates a larger center. Spray with temporary adhesive and center the traced stabilizer over the pile. Sew and finish as usual.

In order to create the necessary stems and leaves I found it easier to actually lay the design out so I could visualize which leaves were the best. Use the illustration below as a guide.

Since the leaves for each flower are the same color, you may save time by hooping and stitching them at the same time. Be sure when tracing the template that you leave at least 1"–2" between the designs.

3. Begin by placing the vase at the bottom center of the back of the garment, and center the large green leaf over the top. Remember to make an allowance for a bottom border when placing the vase. Place the center of the blue flower approximately 15" from the bottom of the vase.

Measure 15" from the bottom of the vase to the center of the tallest flower.

TIP: *General floral design rules suggest that the height of an arrangement should be one to two times the height of the container. In this instance the vase is 6" tall, so the top of the flower should fall somewhere between 12"-18" from the bottom of the vase.*

4. Place the remaining two flowers as shown. Make the stems. One of the great properties of 100% wool is that it tears beautifully, and doesn't fray. For the stems tear $^3/_8$"–$^1/_2$"-wide strips that are 14" long. Don't worry about the length right now. Tuck about 1" of the stem under each flower, bring it down to the center of the vase, and tuck beneath the vase. Since the vase is large, leave the excess stem length under the vase until you're ready to sew. Then trim to approximately 2".

CHOOSING THE LEAF PATTERNS

A florist mixes and matches "greens" to accent a floral design; feel free to do the same. For more variety, use the mirror image of the leaves by placing the traced stabilizer wrong side up. Since I had difficulty selecting the best leaf for my design, I ended up tracing the leaves onto white paper, and played with the cutouts until I was happy with the arrangement. Remember that the finished, sewn designs will be larger than the templates. Tuck the ends of the leaves under the stems.

Since the leaves for each flower are the same color, you may save time by hooping and stitching them at the same time.

TIP: *Be sure when tracing the template that you leave at least 1" between the designs.*

1. Rinse and dry all of the designs. Pin or use temporary adhesive spray to anchor the entire design to the jacket back, and double-check the alignment. Fill in any gaps with additional leaves created by tearing the wool and rounding off the edges. Once the design is set, take a piece of chalk and mark the placement of the three flowers. Remove all of the designs so only the bottom layer of pinned elements remains. In my case this left the three sets of leaves and four torn leaves. This will act as your foundation.

2. Using the invisible polyester thread, stitch each leaf element to the garment. Pin and stitch the stems. For the torn leaves and stems simply stitch down the center of each piece.

3. Place the remaining elements and stitch. I recommend frequently rechecking placement of each design between sewing. Take your time and you'll be rewarded with a stunning floral display!

Novelty Purse

I received a small purse, similar to this one, several years ago and was intrigued with its construction. I turned it inside and out until I had figured out its secret. The construction is extremely easy; just pay attention to the layering and turning instructions. I made the purse to complement the Watercolor Jacket, and used a single flower and the stem from the Flower Wreath Pillow (page 29).

SUPPLIES AND TOOLS

8" square blue wool for the flower
Scrap of brown wool for flower center
One 9" x 14" rectangle green wool for the stem
Fabrics: three fat-quarters of coordinating fabrics—two for the outside of the purse and one for the lining
Felt in coordinating colors for the base of each appliqué
12" x 18" thin cotton batting
45" of cotton cording, or ready-made cording for the strap, or you may construct your own using a 1$^1/_2$" x 45" bias strip of fabric
Optional: brass snap or hook-and-loop tape for closure
Optional: Craft foam to add support and structure
Additional supplies and tools noted in Getting Started (page 5)

INSTRUCTIONS

1. Use the flower pattern (page 55) and stem pattern (page 58) and follow the General Instructions (page 8) to create the flower appliqué. Rinse, dry, and steam press.

2. Cut all four fabrics (including batting) at the same time using a rotary cutter. Stack the four pieces and cut a 10½" x 17" rectangle.

3. If you want to create your own strap, cut a 1½" x 45" strip of fabric. With the wrong side up, fold and press both edges of the purse fabric into the center so they almost meet. Fold the fabric in half, and topstitch.

4. Place the batting down on the table. Then place the tan homespun RIGHT SIDE UP (even though homespuns don't have a right and wrong side it's good to know in case you are using a different fabric).

5. Measure 8¼" from the bottom edge and mark each side. Center each end of the cording or strap over this mark so ¼" extends beyond the edges. Roll up the cord and anchor it with a pin. Place it in the center of the bag, making sure it won't be caught in any of the seam allowances. Baste the cording to the homespun.

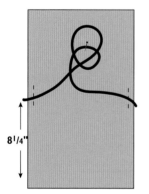

Place ends of cording 8 ¼" from the bottom.

6. Place the pink homespun WRONG SIDE UP over the tan homespun and cording. Fold the bottom edge up to the top so that 1½" of the RIGHT SIDE shows.

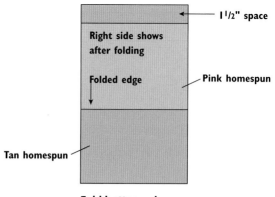

Fold bottom edge up.

7. The edges will not meet—the gap is needed when you turn the purse right side out. The right side of the fabric is now on the outside.

8. With the lining fabric WRONG SIDE UP, trim 1" from one end. Place and align the bottom edge of the lining with the bottom edge of the bag. (There will be a 1" gap at the top.)

9. Pin all layers and stitch a ½"-wide seam around the entire bag. Trim the corners, then trim the seam allowances to ¼".

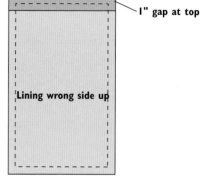

Stitch the ½"-wide seam.

10. The bag is turned twice: First place your hand in the opening of the lining, and pull the outside of the bag through. Push out the corners. Next, grip the inside of the bag and turn it inside out. Push out the corners.

11. Press the bag well. Use the optional craft foam if you want extra support or structure. Cut the craft foam to fit and slip it into the back of the bag. Topstitch ¼" inside all the edges using a complementary color thread, and sewing through the craft foam.

12. Arrange the stem and flower on the outside of the flap, and appliqué in place.

13. If desired, apply a brass snap or hook-and-loop tape to the outside flap underside.

Transform any room into a garden room when you add the Dove Throw and pillow. The soft pastels add a gracious touch to any decor. The throw and pillow also make great gifts for any occasion.

Dove Throw

I was thrilled when I found this cotton lap throw because I liked the lovely pastel print, and decided to coordinate the wool colors with those in the throw. The dove appliqué can be stitched on many types of backgrounds and fabrics. Designs for the dove, heart, and ribbon are included and may be used to create other coordinating projects.

SUPPLIES AND TOOLS

Two 9" x 14" rectangles dark pink wool for doves

Three 9" x 14" rectangles teal wool for center heart and ribbons

One 9" x 14" rectangle olive wool for base

One 9" x 14" rectangle purple wool for tulips

Scraps of pale green for stems and leaves (you will need some 8" lengths for stems)

Felt in coordinating colors for the base of each appliqué

Ready-made cotton throw

Additional supplies and tools noted in Getting Started (see page 5)

INSTRUCTIONS

1. Use the patterns (page 58) and follow the General Instructions (page 8) to create two doves (one is a mirror image of the other), one heart, two tulips, one base, eight ribbons (four are mirror images), and two left tulip leaves (page 56), (one is a mirror image of the other). To make the mirror-image designs trace each design onto the stabilizer and then place the stabilizer WRONG SIDE UP on top of the cutlet pile.

2. Rinse, dry, and trim the felt and ragged edges of cutlets for all of the appliqués.

3. Use the illustration as a placement guide for the appliqués, and arrange the design prior to sewing.

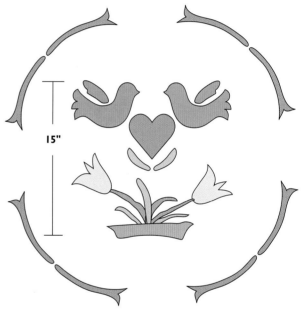

15"

Dove Throw Assembly Diagram

4. Start in the center of the throw and place the heart and two doves. The distance between the base of the tulips and the doves should be approximately 15".

5. Tear ³/₈"-wide strips for the tulip stems, and additional ¹/₂"-wide strips for the leaves, and taper the tops. Place the stems and leaves under the base and tulips.

6. When all designs are in place, arrange the ribbon appliqué to frame the center. Stitch all designs in place with invisible polyester thread.

Flower Wreath Pillow

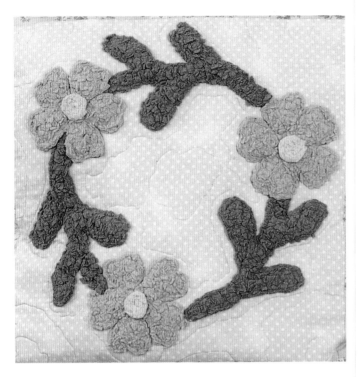

Years ago while going through one of my quilting magazines I saved a photo of a flower wreath quilt by Harriet Hargrave, and pasted it in my "inspirations" notebook. I loved the colors, and the way the flowers intertwined. Although I created different flowers and stems, Harriet's design inspired me!

SUPPLIES AND TOOLS

Two 9" x 14" rectangles dusty pink and medium green wool

Scrap of off-white or celery green for the flower centers

One fat-quarter (18" x 22") cotton for pillow center

$1/2$ yard coordinating blue floral print cotton for the borders and back of pillow

Felt in coordinating colors for the base of each appliqué

20" x 20" muslin for lining

20" x 20" batting

18" pillow form or polyester filling

Universal needle

Additional supplies and tools noted in Getting Started (see page 5)

INSTRUCTIONS

1. Use the flower and stem patterns (page 56) and follow the General Instructions (page 8) to create the three flowers and stem appliqués.

2. Trace all the centers and sew them at one time; remember to leave 1" between each design.

Project note: This finished flower design is a bit tricky, so use a small pair of scissors to cut between the petals.

3. Rinse, dry, and trim the appliqués.

4. With a hand-sewing needle, tack each center to a flower using invisible polyester thread.

5. For the pillow, use a rotary cutter to cut a precise 15" square from the center blue fabric. Cut two 3" x 16" and two 3" x 20" strips from the border fabric.

TIP: *I find it easier to piece borders when you allow a little extra length and trim later.*

6. With right sides together, pin the center square to one of the 16" border strips, leaving $1/4$" of border at the top. Repeat for the opposite side.

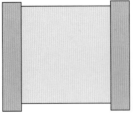

Pin a border strip to each side and stitch.

7. Stitch the pinned borders to the pillow center using a $1/2$"-wide seam. Press the seams toward the strips. Use a rotary cutter and acrylic ruler to square up the edges and trim the excess border fabric from each end.

8. Pin the remaining two border sections to the center fabric, again extend them over each end by $1/2$". Stitch, then press the seams toward the strips. Trim all edges. The top should now measure 19" square.

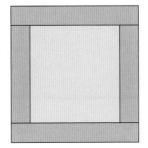

Completed top

19" square

9. Follow the technique for preventing "dog ears" (see page 15). Lay the 20" piece of pressed muslin right side down on a table and place the batting on top. Smooth away wrinkles. Fold back half of the batting and lightly spray with temporary adhesive. Replace the batting over the muslin, and smooth away wrinkles. Fold back the remaining half of batting, spray, and press onto the muslin. Center the tapered 19" pillow top over the batting, and repeat the spraying process.

10. Arrange the appliqués on the center of the pillow top. The stems and flowers should connect in a ring. Stitch all designs in place with invisible polyester thread.

11. When you are pleased with the arrangement, use a water-soluble marker and draw an outline ¹/₂" away from each design. Since the designs form a ring, you'll draw a continuous line inside the wreath, and then another one outside the wreath. These lines become the quilting lines.

12. Draw (free-hand) lines that echo the appliquéd designs. Draw a flower and its center in each of the four corners. I drew a squiggly circle in the center of the pillow and a long, irregularly shaped oblong circle along each edge. *None of the lines should encroach in the ¹/₂"-wide seam allowance.*

Quilting lines repeat the appliqué shapes.

13. Remove the appliqués from the pillow top. Pin the layers of the top together every 6–8". Make sure none of the pins cross the quilting lines.

14. Set up your machine with a size 75 Universal needle and invisible polyester thread on top. The bobbin thread should match the fabric.

TIP: *If your machine has a needle-down option, use it here. If you have a walking foot, use it to prevent the layers from shifting.*

15. Stitch on the quilting lines. When you've finished quilting the top, pin the rag wool designs onto the pillow top. Use a Jeans/Denim needle and stitch the designs to the pillow top using invisible polyester thread.

16. Trim the excess batting and muslin, using the top as a pattern. Zigzag or serge the layers together along all edges.

17. Place a 20" square of the backing fabric right side up on your table. With right sides together, center the top over the back. Pin all edges. Use the top as a pattern to trim the excess backing fabric.

18. On one edge, mark two Xs, 6" apart for the opening. The opening will allow you to stuff the pillow. Starting at one of the Xs, stitch the layers together, using a ¹/₂"-wide seam allowance. Stop stitching at the other X. Backstitch at the beginning and at the end. Clip the four corners close to the seam and turn the pillow right side out.

19. For nice, pointed corners, working from the inside of the pillow, use the eraser end of a pencil to push out the four corners. Press the corners. Turn under the seam allowance of the opening and press.

20. Insert the pillow form (or fill with loose filling). Slipstitch the opening closed.

Fall is my favorite time of year in New England. The rich warm colors of the fall harvest inspire my decorating scheme, so these projects are the perfect complement.

Frost on the Pumpkin Wallhanging
Finished size: 11" x 26"

One of my favorites of hand-dyed wool that I carry is "Frost on the Pumpkin," which is available in muted bronzey oranges (see Resources on page 63). Each of the three pumpkins was created from a different value of this wool. Don't they evoke autumn?

Other than assembling the rag wool pumpkins, and making a few stitches to tack them on, there is little sewing involved. Because prewashed wool does not ravel when it is torn, and homespuns tear straight on the grain, this project was completed in just minutes using an iron-on adhesive. The grapevines came from the woods near my home, and made a great hanger.

SUPPLIES AND TOOLS

Three 9" x 14" rectangles muted orange wool (three different shades works well)

One 9" x 14" rectangle dark green for the stems

One 9" x 14" rectangle black wool for border (I used a hand-dyed mottled black)

$1/4$ yard or 8" x 24" beige wool or homespun for the center section

$1/3$ yard or 12" x 28" of homespun fabric in a complementary color

Black felt for backing: Approximately $1/2$ yard

Felt in coordinating colors for the base of each appliqué

$1 1/2$ yards of paper-backed iron-on adhesive (such as Heat-N-Bond Ultrahold®)

Four 26"-long pieces of grapevine or twigs, and floral wire to create the hanger

Additional supplies and tools noted in Getting Started (see page 5)

INSTRUCTIONS

1. Use the pumpkin and stem patterns (page 59) and follow the General Instructions (page 8) to create the three different pumpkin appliqués using a different color wool for each one. The three stem designs can be sewn at the same time; remember to leave 1" between each design.

TIP: *Do not trim any ragged edges at this time.*

2. Tear or cut the wool and homespun before you start assembling the project. Before tearing wool or homespun, snip $1/2$" into the edge of the fabric, then rip.

3. Tear a 12" x 28" piece of wool or homespun for the center section. Also tear an 8" x 24" piece. Cut a 13" x 29" piece of black felt for the back of the wallhanging. Cut pieces of iron-on adhesive 12" x 28" and $7 1/2$" x $23 1/2$".

4. Lay the 13" x 29" piece of backing felt on the ironing board and center the 12" x 28" iron-on adhesive on top, paper side facing up. There should be a $1/2$" border of felt around all edges. Fuse the adhesive to the felt.

TIP: Note: *Follow the manufacturer's instructions for iron settings and pressing time when using any of the iron-on adhesives. Always take a minute and practice on a scrap first!*

← $1/2$"

Iron-on adhesive centered over felt

5. Cut an $11 1/2$" x $27 1/2$" piece from this bonded felt. Remove the paper backing.

6. Before applying the felt to the homespun, make sure the homespun is well pressed, and that the corners are square. You might need to tug a little here and there to straighten the grain. Once the felt is fused you'll no longer have this luxury!

7. Place the 12" x 28" homespun wrong side up on the ironing board, and center the black felt, **adhesive side down**, so there is a $^1/_4$" of homespun showing on all edges. Fuse the felt to the homespun.

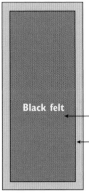

Black felt

→ **Bonded felt**

→ **Homespun**

Homespun extends $^1/_4$" beyond the feltedges.

8. Pull away several strands of thread along each side of the homespun to create a ragged appearance.

9. Place the 8" x 24" wool center section on the ironing board and center the iron-on adhesive, **paper side up**, so there is a $^1/_4$" border. Fuse to the wool, and remove the paper backing.

Iron-on adhesive centered over wool

10. Center the wool over the homespun, adhesive side down, so a 2" border of homespun shows on all edges. Fuse the wool to the homespun.

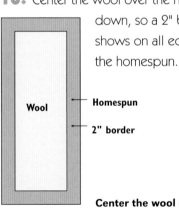

Wool

→ **Homespun**

→ **2" border**

Center the wool over the homespun.

11. Position the border along the edge where the wool and homespun meet. Tear sufficient $^3/_4$"-wide pieces of wool to go around the entire border. (The lengths of these pieces are determined by the size of your wool.) Place the lengths end-to-end. Be sure to stagger the points where the strips meet.

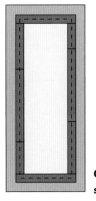

Center the border strips over the top and stagger the lengths.

12. When you are pleased with the arrangement of your border, cut $^1/_4$" strips of iron-on adhesive and apply to the center of each border length. Fuse the border sections to the wallhanging; firmly press each edge into each other to blend the join.

APPLYING THE PUMPKINS

Before attaching the pumpkins and stems, trim the edges, except **leave the area ragged where the stem and pumpkin join**. Tack each pumpkin in two or three places. Place the stem up against the pumpkin and tack in place using the smoke-colored invisible polyester thread. Stitch all designs in place with invisible polyester thread.

GRAPEVINE HANGER

For the hanger use four 26"-long grapevine strands and tie them together with floral wire. Using an awl or scissors, poke a hole through the wallhanging $^1/_4$" in from each side and $^1/_2$" down from the top edge. Poke a third hole in the center $^1/_2$" down from the top edge. Use $^1/_2$"-wide torn strips of wool to attach the wallhanging to the grapevine; strips of homespun would also work. Thread pieces through the holes, tie to the grapevine, and adjust the ties so the fabric portion hangs straight.

Autumn Harvest No-Sew Feed-Sack Pillow

As much as I love to sew and create, sometimes there is not enough time in the day. I began making these feed sack pillows several years ago when I was in a frantic rush to complete projects for a trade show. With a yard of fabric and twine, I whipped up several samples in just minutes! Other than creating and tacking the rag wool designs in place, no sewing is involved. This Autumn Harvest pillow is a perfect complement to the Frost on the Pumpkin project.

SUPPLIES AND TOOLS

Three 9" x 14" rectangles muted orange wool (three different shades)

One 9" x 14" rectangle dark green for the stems and large leaf

1 1/3 yards coordinating homespun

Felt in coordinating colors for the base of each appliqué

14" pillow form

Double-stick tape

Jute twine

Additional supplies and tools noted in Getting Started (page 5)

INSTRUCTIONS

Use the pumpkin and stem patterns (page 59), and the leaf template from the Watercolor Jacket project (page 54), and follow the General Instructions (page 8) to create three pumpkins.

CREATING THE PILLOW WRAP

1. Tear or cut a piece of homespun to measure 30" x 45" width of fabric; press smooth and lay out on a table, wrong side up.

2. Center the pillow form on top of the homespun, with the center of the pillow 3"– 4" below the center of the homespun.

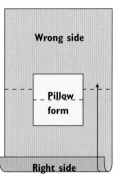

3. Bring up the bottom edge of the homespun and wrap it around the pillow until it reaches the top of the pillow form.

4. Fold the top half of the fabric over the pillow form.

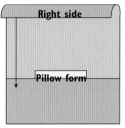

Bring the top half over the pillow.

5. At the center of the pillow, fold under the raw edge (just like you would wrap a present). Temporarily tape the fabric closed along this edge using double-stick tape. Gather each side of the fabric and tie securely with jute twine.

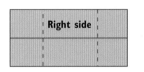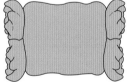

Gather along the sides of the pillow form.

6. Once both sides are tied, adjust the gathers so they are even, pulling the fabric to make it taut. The jute ties should be equidistant from the pillow center.

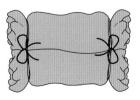

Adjust gathers

7. Arrange the pumpkins and large leaf on top of the pillow, overlapping the pumpkins slightly and placing the large leaf along the bottom edge. Secure using double-stick tape.

8. Carefully remove the pillow form. Use invisible polyester thread to tack or appliqué each pumpkin and leaf to the homespun.

9. Reinsert the pillow form. If you'd like, stuff a bit of loose batting in each side under the tied area to fill the pillow out a bit more. Once you're satisfied with each side, make 1" snips along the edges of the gathered fabric. Tear the homespun all the way to the twine ties. This creates a tasseled look, and allows the ends to hang.

Black-Eyed Susan Table Runner

Finished size approximately 17" x 40"

This table runner was created from a series of hand-dyed wools called "Black-Eyed Susan" (see Resources on page 63). The rich tones of gold and yellow brought the flowers to life and gave them more dimension. For the borders and center I chose a mottled black hand-dyed wool that had some hints of gold. For this project I used a mitering technique inspired by my carpenter.

SUPPLIES AND TOOLS

$1/2$ yard (56" wide) gold wool for petals (you may combine several shades of gold)

$1/4$ yard (56" wide) black wool for centers and borders

1 yard gold felt and scraps of black felt for the base of the appliqués

$1/2$ yard gold striped homespun for backgrounds

$5/8$ yard gold checked homespun for back and binding

40" x 20" cotton batting

Additional supplies and tools noted in Getting Started (see page 5)

INSTRUCTIONS

1. From the black wool, cut 3"-wide strips for the borders before you make the cutlets. Piece the border strips (see page 15 for piecing borders). The total length required is 148". From that length cut two 3" x 12" and two 3" x 18" strips. Set aside the remainder of the border length.

2. Make the cutlets and the three black centers (I also sprinkled a few gold cutlets in each center) from the remaining black wool.

3. Use the patterns (page 52) and follow the General Instructions (page 8) to create 18 gold flower petals. If you choose you may make two petals at one time. Be sure to leave 1" between the petals.

4. Trim the ragged edges of the cutlets on the flower petals. Leave the edges of the center circles untrimmed for now.

5. Cut three $11^1/2$" x $11^1/2$" squares from the striped homespun.

6. Center a 3" x 12" border strip on each side of one of the $11^1/2$" squares, allowing a slight overlap at each end. With right sides together, stitch using a $1/2$"-wide seam

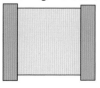 allowance. Press toward the homespun. Trim the excess border fabric from each end.

The borders extend beyond each end.

7. Sew a square to the other side of each border. Press and trim. The rectangle should measure $36^1/2$" x $11^1/2$".

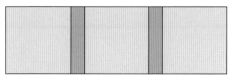

Borders trimmed even with the squares.

8. Center a 3" x 18" border strip at each end of the runner. With right sides together, stitch using a $^1/_2$"-wide seam allowance. Press seam flat.

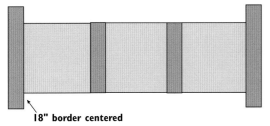

18" border centered

Do not trim the excess border length. It is needed to create the mitered border!

TIP: *Note: I used hand-dyed wool for the border. When using wool, which tends to "stretch," it's difficult to get perfectly crisp corners or miters. This is the nature of the beast, and will become part of the project's "charm." Try the Carpenter's Mitering technique. You might like it.*

CARPENTER'S MITER

My carpenter created such perfect inside corners with wood molding that I asked him to share his trick. I adapted his technique to miter corners.

1. Place the top, right side up, on the ironing board. Cut the remaining border length in half. Take one of the remaining long border lengths and place it right sides together with the top so the borders create a 90° angle with the edges even.

Right side
Top
Wrong side

Sewn border pressed open

Place border right sides together along the bottom edge to create a 90° angle.

2. Fold the bottom right corner of the border so its side edge is perfectly even with the top. A 45° angle is created along the fold. Repeat the mitering process for the remaining three corners.

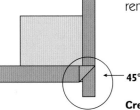

45°

Create a 45° angle along the fold.

3. You'll notice that a small area of background fabric is visible, which creates a small triangle. At the tip of this triangle is the intersection of the seam allowance and the folded border. Begin sewing the $^1/_2$"-wide seam at the intersection of the seam allowance and the folded edge.

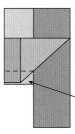

Close-up of intersection between the seam allowance and the folded border

4. Pin the border to the top. Beginning at the intersection, stitch the border to the background. Do not stitch past the intersection into the border, or the miter will not form properly.

5. Fold open the border. Trim the excess border so the bottom edges are even. Edge-stitch the fold of the miter so it lays flat.

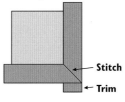

Stitch

Trim

Trim excess and edge stitch the fold.

6. Lay the top on a piece of cotton batting; use it as a pattern to cut the batting to fit the top's dimension.

7. Place the batting and top on the piece of gold-checked homespun (wrong side up) so there is at least 2" on all edges. Pin the three layers together.

8. Trim the backing to 1$^1/_2$". Fold the edge of the backing in half to meet the top edge. Press. Fold over to the top. This will create a $^3/_4$" binding. Pin in place. From the top, edge-stitch close to the folded edge using the invisible polyester thread.

9. Use the instructions from the Blooming Posy Fleece Jacket (page 40) to create the three flowers. Sew a center to each flower. Center a flower in each panel, and either tack or appliqué the edges to the table runner.

Timmy's Tree Star Vest

This beautiful star has special meaning to me. One day, when my youngest son was three years old, he was playing with a bag of rejected rag wool trees. He was happy, and I was thrilled to have a few minutes to sew. Suddenly Timmy yelled, "Look Mommy, it's a tree star." The little darling had arranged eight trees into this beautiful pattern. He inspired me! Motifs can be combined to create new designs. I've modified it a little, but it's still "Timmy's Tree Star." When completed, the design is approximately 10" x 9", making it the perfect size for the back of a jacket or vest.

SUPPLIES AND TOOLS

Four 9" x 14" rectangles gold wool

$1/4$ yard coordinating gold felt for the base of each appliqué

Double-stick tape

Purchased vest or jacket

Additional supplies and tools noted in Getting Started (page 5)

When choosing items to decorate, I always try to find things rich in texture. Berber fleece, with its nubby surface, complements the rag wool appliqués perfectly! I used the faux chenille technique to create the textured tote bag.

INSTRUCTIONS

1. Use the patterns (page 60) and follow the General Instructions (page 8) to create the following elements: one piece A, two pieces B, two pieces BR, two pieces C, and two pieces D.

2. In a hot dryer, tumble-dry all the appliqués together.

TIP: *It is very important that you leave 1" of felt around each design. Do not trim any of the ragged edges of the cutlets.*

JOINING THE DESIGNS

Join the design elements using the technique outlined in the General Instructions (page 14). Be sure you understand the piecing technique before proceeding. Use the illustration below as a guide.

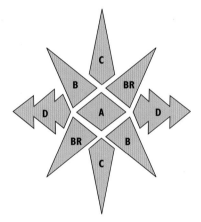

Diagram for Timmy's Tree

1. Begin by creating the "lips" on all edges of piece A.

2. For the four B/BR pieces, remove the felt only along the short edge that will be connected to piece A. Leave excess felt on the remaining two sides for the next round of piecing.

3. Using the double-stick tape as described in the General Instructions, attach and stitch the B pieces.

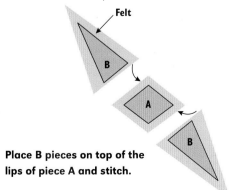

Place B pieces on top of the lips of piece A and stitch.

Join the two sections together so the ragged cutlets blend into each other. Check frequently that the lines are intersecting. The star should now look like the star shown below.

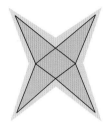

Completed center section

4. Create a ½" felt lip as shown below. The felt B and BR pieces overlap, creating a new lip.

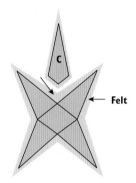

Place each section onto the new lip and stitch.

5. Treat the remaining four pieces of C and D as you did before by trimming the felt close to the stitching line. Follow the piecing technique and stitch to the edges of pieces B and BR.

6. Once the design is fully pieced, trim all felt edges close to the stitching lines. At this point stitch over the seams joining the design elements with a narrow zigzag stitch and invisible polyester thread.

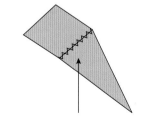

Zigzag over the adjoining seam.

7. Trim any ragged cutlets to redefine the edge. Spray the back of the star with temporary adhesive, and pin to the jacket back.

8. Stitch to the jacket by sewing along the outside edge, over the previous stitching. For extra support stitch the center diamond to the jacket.

Pinwheel Vest

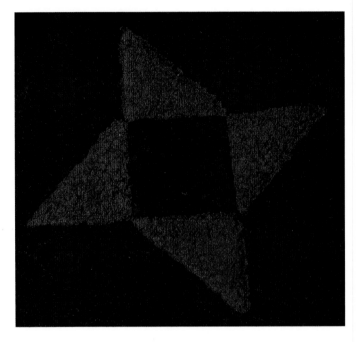

Like the Blue Suede Jacket project (page 22), this design is based on a simple quilt block combination. Using just two geometric shapes you can create a dramatic design. For this vest I used the 4" pinwheel on the back, and placed the coordinating 2" pinwheel on the upper left front. The texture of the black fleece vest complements the designs beautifully.

SUPPLIES AND TOOLS

Three 9" x 14" rectangles (¼ yard) deep orange wool

One 9" x 14" rectangle black wool

Felt in coordinating colors for the base of each appliqué

Ready-made vest or jacket

Additional supplies and tools noted in Getting Started
   (page 5)

INSTRUCTIONS

1. Use the patterns (page 57) and follow the General Instructions (page 8) to create one 4" black square and four 2" half-square triangles in the deep orange. For the front of the jacket, create one 2" black square and four coordinating 2" half-square triangles.

TIP: *Do not trim any of the ragged edges, and make sure to leave 1" of felt around all edges.*

2. Like other projects that require design piecing, join sections prior to appliquéing them to the vest or jacket. There are two ways to piece these elements together: Follow the General Instructions (page 14) or use the technique described in the Blue Suede Jacket project (page 22). If you choose the technique in the General Instructions, join the sections with a narrow zigzag stitch.

3. Begin by sewing a triangle to sides opposite of the square. Repeat for the remaining two triangles.

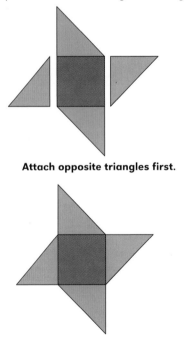

Attach opposite triangles first.

4. The front and back designs are pieced exactly the same way. When pieced, trim the felt close to the stitching line, and trim the ragged edges of the cutlets.

5. Spray the back of the pinwheel with temporary adhesive, and pin to the jacket.

6. Use invisible polyester thread to stitch the pinwheel to the garment.

Blooming Posy Fleece Jacket

This jacket can almost make a cold winter day seem like spring! The blue and black flowers are a pretty addition to the oatmeal fleece. I added the black wool background to prevent the flower from "floating in space," and to coordinate it with the black collar ribbing. Choose a fleece jacket vest that you like, wools in pretty colors, and create a design original.

SUPPLIES AND TOOLS

Six 9" x 14" rectangles blue wool (I used a combination of three shades of blue.)

$1/3$ yard black wool for the background and center

Felt in coordinating colors for the base of each appliqué

Ready-made jacket or vest

Additional supplies and tools noted in Getting Started (page 5)

INSTRUCTIONS

1. Use the petal patterns (page 52) and follow the General Instructions (page 8) to create six petals from the Black-Eyed Susan pattern.

2. Trim the felt and all ragged edges of wool.

3. Trim $1/2$" off of the top of **one end** of each petal.

Trim petals.

4. Place the trimmed ends together.

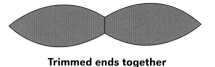

Trimmed ends together

5. Use a Jeans/Denim needle and any color all-purpose sewing thread. These stitches do not have to be invisible. If you have the zigzag feature, use a wide zigzag stitch to stitch across the joined edges.

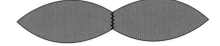

Repeat this procedure for the other two pairs of petals.

6. Tear a 12" square from the black wool. Arrange the petals in the center of the wool so the centers intersect. Pin the petals in place.

7. Stitch along the outside edge of each petal with invisible polyester thread, then stitch toward the center. The flower gets very thick toward the center, and might not accommodate the height of your presser foot. Sew in as far as you're able; you'll be able to get close enough.

8. Use the circle template (page 52) to cut a piece of black wool. Stitch the circle to the center of the flower. If necessary, tack the center down by hand.

9. **Tear** the excess wool away from all sides of the background square so there is only $3/4$" from the top and bottom petals.

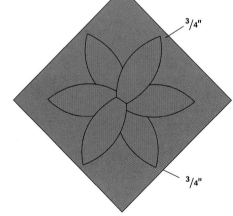

10. Center the wool on the jacket back and stitch $1/2$" inside the edge of the wool. Echo stitch the outline of the flower to help secure the panel.

Faux Chenille Quilted Tote Bag

Tote bags are a great accessory and offer a wonderful opportunity to try new sewing techniques. The pattern included here is actually a compilation of many of the different patterns and techniques I've learned over the years. This tote bag project features the faux chenille technique along with rag wool appliqué designs on one side; the opposite side is machine quilted. Also included is a neat trick for creating a "built-in binding" from the lining fabric.

SUPPLIES AND TOOLS

Three 9" x 14" rectangles dark red wool

$5/8$ yard each of four different pieces of coordinating 100% cotton fabric (I used flannel.)

Felt in coordinating colors for the base of each appliqué

$3/4$ yard striped fabric for lining, handle, and binding

$1/2$ yard muslin

$1/2$ yard cotton batting

Five $3/4$" wood buttons

Craft paper (for the tote bag pattern), two 20" x 24" pieces

Jute twine

Additional supplies and tools noted in Getting Started (page 5)

INSTRUCTIONS

Use the diamond pattern from the Rabbit project (page 61) and follow the General Instructions (page 8) to create six diamonds.

TIP: *You may trim all ragged edges of the wool.*

CREATING THE FAUX CHENILLE PANEL

1. Use rotary tools to cut the four different flannels into 18" x 22" rectangles. Stack the rectangles on top of each other with all right sides facing up. **Trim $1/4$" from each edge** of the top **three** layers of the fabric to aid in the future slashing process (you may eyeball this). Lightly spray between each layer with the temporary adhesive to prevent shifting of the layers. Smooth the fabrics so there are no wrinkles.

2. Use your long 24" acrylic ruler and a water-soluble marking pen to draw a 45° bias line on the top layer. Use the first line as a guide and draw parallel lines $1/2$" apart to cover the entire top.

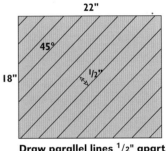

Draw parallel lines $1/2$" apart.

3. Set up your sewing machine with all-purpose sewing thread that matches the top layer of fabric. Use the same thread in the bobbin.

4. Use a straight stitch and a walking foot (if you have one) and stitch on each drawn line.

5. Slashing the faux chenille: Use a pair of sharp scissors to cut the **top three layers of fabric between the sewing lines. Do not cut through the bottom layer of fabric.**

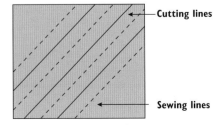

Cut through the top three layers.

6. When you are finished cutting, stitch around all sides with a zigzag stitch. Wash the layered, slashed fabric in the washing machine, and dry completely in a hot dryer. This will cause the fabric to "bloom."

CREATING THE QUILTED BACKING

1. To add body and to balance the heaviness of the faux chenille front, I found it necessary to make a quilted back. Layer 16" x 19" pieces of muslin, batting, and flannel (right side up).

2. Spray the layers as you did for the faux chenille panel (step 1). You may quilt this any way you like (your favorite quilting pattern). The purpose of this step is to hold the layers together. For this project a 4" grid was drawn, on the bias, using an acrylic ruler and water-soluble marker. Using the grid as a guide, stitch with matching thread. Use a walking foot if you have one.

CREATING THE TOTE BAG PATTERN

The tote bag is basically a rectangle with two notches cut out at the bottom corners. Use craft paper for the pattern.

1. Use a 24" acrylic ruler to cut a 15" x 18" paper rectangle. Fold the rectangle in half lengthwise so it measures 9" x 15".

2. Remove a 2 1/2" square from the bottom corner.

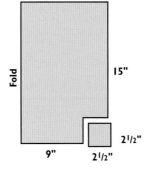

3. Open the paper; the pattern should look like the illustration below.

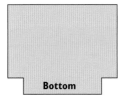

Tote Bag Pattern

CONSTRUCTING THE TOTE BAG

At this point you should have the quilted back and the faux chenille ready for construction. Because the layers are thick, you need to cut them separately.

1. Center the pattern piece over the quilted back, keeping the fabric grain straight. Pin and cut the back.

2. The chenille's bias cuts make it stretchy, so you will need to add a layer of muslin to the back of the faux chenille to stabilize it. Place a 16" x 19" piece of muslin down first, and lightly spray with temporary adhesive. Center the faux chenille (right side up), followed by the pattern. Pin all layers and cut the top.

3. With right sides together, pin the front and back pieces together along the bottom edge. Sew the bottom together using a 1/2"-wide seam. Press the seam open.

4. With right sides together, pin side seams. Stitch 1/2"-wide seam, and press open. At this point the two corners should still be open.

5. The side and bottom seams are brought together and sewn to create the bottom shape of the bag.

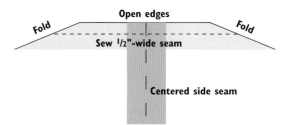

Bring the side and bottom seams together and stitch.

With right sides together, align the side seam with the bottom seam. The raw edges will match. Pin and sew a 1/2"-wide seam. Repeat for the other side. Turn the bag right side out, and use the eraser end of a pencil to "push out" the corners.

6. The lining pattern is slightly different because of the built-in binding. Use a new piece of craft paper and cut a 16" x 18" rectangle, then fold it in half so it measures 16" x 9". Measure and remove the 2 1/2" square from the corner. Pin, then cut two pieces from lining fabric using the new pattern.

7. Construct the lining following steps 3–5 above, except leave a 6" opening in the bottom center seam for turning.

8. With right sides together, place the outer bag inside the lining, matching side seams. Pin along the top raw edges. Stitch a 1/2"-wide seam. Stitch again 1/4" away from the raw edges. Pull the two bags apart (they are still inside out), and **press the seam toward the lining.**

9. Turn the bag right side out through the hole in the lining. With wrong sides together, bring the edges of the open bottom seam together and stitch with a 1/8"-wide seam.

10. Push the lining fabric down into the bag. Wrap the lining around the top 1/2"-wide seam allowance; this will create the illusion of the binding. Topstitch in the seam groove through all thicknesses.

HANDLES

1. Cut two 2 1/2" x 25" pieces each of lining and cotton batting. Place a strip of batting on the wrong side of the lining fabric. Fold each strip in half, right sides together, and pin along the 25" side. Sew together using a 1/4"-wide seam. Trim the batting close to the seam allowance. Turn the handle right side out. Press each handle so the seam is centered.

2. Tuck the raw edges of the handle ends under 1/2". You may find it helpful to remove a little of the batting. Press the ends. Using matching thread, topstitch 1/4" away from all edges.

3. The handles are attached to the outside of the bag. Measure 5 1/2" in from each side seam of the tote bag and place a pin there. Place the wrong side of the handle on the right side of the bag so the handle is centered over the pin, leaving a 1" overlap on the bag. Stitch the handles in place by sewing a square.

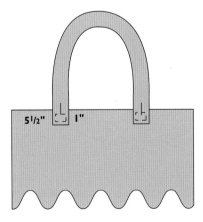

4. Thread each end of a 4" piece of thin twine through the buttons from the back. Pull so the lengths are even. Center the button over the end of the handle and pin the twine up and away from the holes. Sew the buttons to the bag, making sure the twine is out of the way. Tie the twine in a square knot, and trim the ends to 1/2". Place a dab of craft glue on each end of twine and on the knot to prevent fraying.

APPLYING THE APPLIQUÉS TO THE TOTE BAG

Pin the faux chenille to the lining in several areas so the lining doesn't shift. Pin the rag wool appliqués to the faux chenille front, and stitch using the invisible polyester thread.

I designed this so all of the diamond points meet in the center, then added a button.

Optional: Cover a 4 1/2" x 13" piece of craft foam with coordinating lining fabric, and place in the bottom of the bag for stability and to make it look more structured.

Leaping Rabbits

American folk art fans are sure to recognize the handsome silhouette in these projects. Leaping rabbits can be found in hand-hooked rugs, on weathervanes, and now, appliquéd to the back of a ready-made jacket (page 47), on a rustic pillow, and, along with the Bear Paw quilt motif, on the top of a cozy Northwoods-style lap throw.

Sometimes when you don't follow the rules, wonderful things can happen! The medium-brown wool in the pillow and lap throw was a pleasant surprise because the wool prewashed and dried into a beautifully textured background for the appliqués. Purchase extra wool to allow for shrinkage during prewashing. Prewash the wool first to allow for shrinkage. Remember, too, that in the wash-and-dry process, the fabric may be pulled off grain; make necessary adjustments as you sew to be sure your corners are square.

Rabbit Lap Throw

Finished size: 46" x 72"

SUPPLIES AND TOOLS

Three 9" x 14" rectangles tan and white houndstooth-check wool for rabbits and small squares

$3/4$ yard dark brown wool for squares

$3/4$ yard dark green wool for triangles

1" x 1" black felt for each rabbit's eyes

Felt in coordinating colors for the base of each appliqué

$2^{1}/4$ yards of 54"–60"-wide wool or other fabric for background

$2^{1}/4$ yards dark charcoal fleece for backing and binding

Double-stick tape

Additional supplies and tools noted in Getting Started (page 5)

INSTRUCTIONS

1. Use the rabbit patterns (page 61) and follow the General Instructions (page 8) to create two hounds-tooth-check rabbits, adding a black felt eye about $1/4$" in diameter to each one.

2. Use the patterns (page 61) to make 72 dark green 2" triangles, 18 dark brown 4" squares, and 4 tan and white houndstooth-check 2" squares. On the rabbits and 2" squares, trim the felt edges and any ragged cutlets.

3. Follow the piecing technique described in the General Instructions (page 14) and use one 4" square and four 2" triangles (page 57) to assemble each Bear Paw. Make 18 Paw units. For each one, create the lip of felt on the 4" square. Attach the triangles as described in the General Instructions (page 14) using invisible polyester thread and narrow zigzag stitches. Finish the units by trimming the felt and ragged wool cutlets.

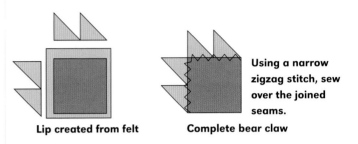

Lip created from felt   **Complete bear claw**   Using a narrow zigzag stitch, sew over the joined seams.

4. Cut the top piece of wool or fabric to 48" x 74".

5. Use a chalk pencil or water-soluble marker to draw a large crosshair in the center of the lap throw fabric. Piece and sew the design from the center of this line outward.

6. Place a piece of double-stick tape on the back of each design element. Position the rabbits in the center of the crosshairs. Place a single Bear Paw on each side of each rabbit so that the horizontal line intersects as shown.

7. Draw a chalk line 6" above and below the Paw. There is a 4" space between each of the large Bear Paw clusters. Draw a line 2" on each side of the centerline to mark the boundaries for the clusters.

8. Use the drawn boundaries to place the Bear Paw units. Position the trimmed houndstooth square in the center of four units. Use this square to align the Paws and to ensure that there is 2" between them.

9. When you are pleased with the positioning, use invisible polyester thread to stitch the elements to the top. Begin by sewing the rabbits and single Bear Paws. Before continuing, recheck the placement of the next pieces. Stitch all design elements in place.

10. Pin through all layers around each houndstooth square. Check the back of the lap throw to ensure that there are no wrinkles, then sew over the previously stitched edges of the small squares to secure the front of the throw to the back.

11. To create the binding using fabrics other than fleece, lay the backing wrong side up on the floor, and center the top over the backing. Trim the backing, leaving a 4" border beyond the top. Bind, using the technique described with the Tea-Dyed Flowerpot Table Rug project (see page 20).

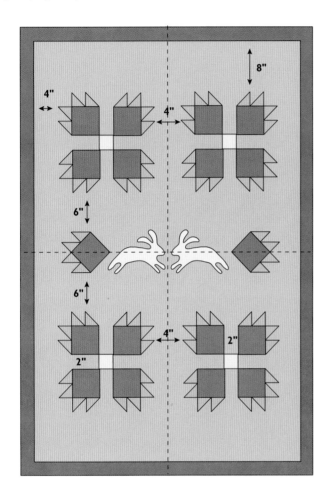

Rabbit Pillow

Finished size: 16" x 20"

If you make the lap throw, consider making at least one pillow to complement it.

SUPPLIES AND TOOLS

One 9" x 14" rectangle tan and white houndstooth-check wool for the rabbit

Three 9" x 14" rectangles dark brown wool for diamonds

One 9" x 14" rectangle dark green wool for triangles

1" x 1" black felt for rabbit's eye

3/4 yard medium brown wool for pillow front and back

Felt in coordinating colors for the base of each appliqué

Pillow form or polyester fiberfill

Additional supplies and tools noted in Getting Started (page 5)

INSTRUCTIONS

1. Use the rabbit, diamond, and triangle patterns (page 61) and follow the General Instructions (page 8) to create one rabbit, six brown diamonds, and six green triangles. Appliqué a small, circular eye to the rabbit's head; trim excess felt. Trim and clip the felt and ragged cutlets.

2. Cut two 21" x 17" pieces of wool for the pillow front and back.

3. Use a water-soluble marker or chalk pencil to draw a 16" x 12" rectangle in the center of the pillow front. Taper the edges to prevent dog-eared corners (see page 15).

4. Refer to the illustration opposite and place the triangles, diamonds, and rabbit on the pillow top. Note that the points of the triangles and diamonds do not extend beyond the drawn rectangle, which keeps the design on top of the pillow after it is stuffed. Pin; using invisible polyester thread, stitch the designs to the top.

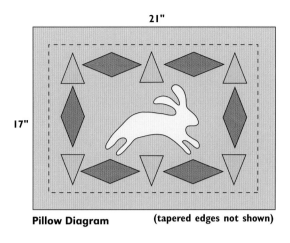

Pillow Diagram (tapered edges not shown)

5. With right sides together, pin and stitch the front and back pillow pieces together using a $1/2$"-wide seam. Leave a 6" opening along the bottom. Trim corners. Turn the pillow right side out, and fill it with a pillow form or stuffing. Slipstitch the opening closed.

Rabbit Jacket

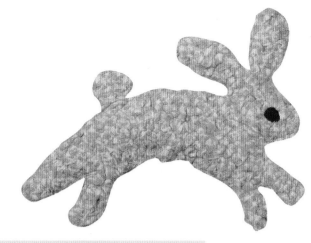

SUPPLIES AND TOOLS

One 9" x 14" rectangle tan and white houndstooth-check wool for the rabbit

One 9" x 14" rectangle dark brown wool for diamonds

6" x 6" dark green wool for triangle

1" x 1" black felt for rabbit's eye

Felt in coordinating colors for the base of each appliqué

Ready-made jacket

Additional supplies and tools noted in Getting Started (page 5)

INSTRUCTIONS

1. Use the rabbit, diamond, and triangle patterns (page 61) and follow the General Instructions (page 8) to create one rabbit, two brown diamonds, and one green triangle. Appliqué a small, circular eye about $1/4$" in diameter to the rabbit's head; trim excess felt.

2. Trim and clip the felt and ragged cutlets.

3. Position the appliqués on the back of the jacket. Pin; using invisible polyester thread, sew each element in place.

Jacket placement

Sweet Kids

The projects in Sweet Kids and Sports Kids (see page 50) take advantage of ready-made items, and are very simple. Place the designs on items that won't need frequent washings, such as jacket backs, bags, and blankets. You might want to embellish a peg rack for a children's room. The baseball and basketball appliqués use the same circle, but have different finishing details. Create 2" versions of these balls by using the center pattern from the Black-Eyed Susan Table Runner (page 52). Use your imagination. The possibilities are unlimited!

SUPPLIES AND TOOLS

For each project:

Felt in coordinating colors for the base of each appliqué

Yarn or thin strips of wool for the details (such as lacing on football or baseball)

Additional supplies and tools noted in Getting Started (page 5)

Sailboat: 8" squares of two contrasting colors of wool

Angel: Two 8" squares for body and wings
    Wool scrap for head and feet

Tulip: 8" squares of two coordinating colors of wool

With the exception of the angel, trim all ragged edges of the cutlets after the appliqués are complete.

1. Use the patterns on pages 51 and 62 and follow the General Instructions (page 8) to create the design of your choice. For the tulip jacket, use the tulip from the flowerpot patterns (page 56), and tear a piece of wool for the stem.

2. Trim and clip the felt and ragged cutlets. (**Do NOT do this for the Angel.**)

3. Position the appliqués on the back of the vest or jacket. Pin, and use invisible polyester thread to stitch the appliqué in place.

Angel: After making the appliqués, apply the angel's body with the invisible polyester thread. Trim the wool along the edges where the head, feet, and wings WILL NOT be joined. Next, position the remaining appliqués, and stitch in place with invisible polyester thread.

Combine appliqués with machine embroidered letters.

Baseball, Basketball, or Football

One 9" x 14" rectangle of wool for each design

Yarn or thin strips of wool for the details (such as lacing on football or baseball)

Felt in coordinating colors for the base of each appliqué

Additional supplies and tools noted in Getting Started
   (page 5)

Create the appliqué of your choice.

1. Use the baseball, basketball, or football patterns and follow the General Instructions (page 8) to create the appliqué of your choice.

2. Trim the felt and ragged cutlets after the appliqués are complete.

3. Add the details as suggested in the patterns, such as the laces on the football.

Note: The detail patterns are not to scale, but serve only as a guide. Use invisible polyester thread to attach the thin wool strips or yarn to the finished appliqué.

4. Position the appliqué on the back of the vest or jacket. Pin and use invisible polyester thread to stitch the design in place.

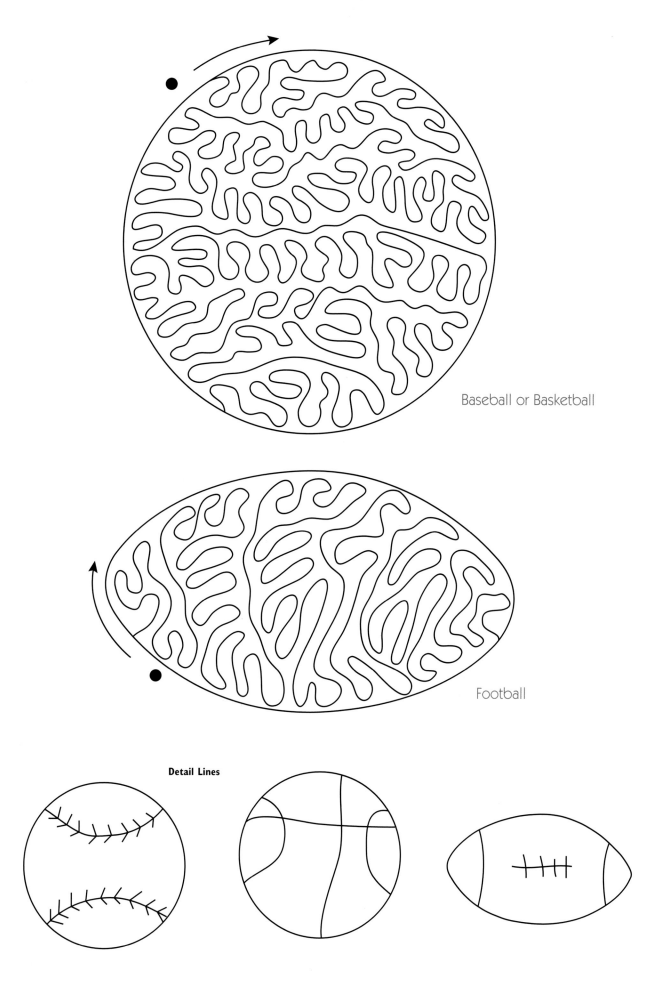

Baseball or Basketball

Football

Detail Lines

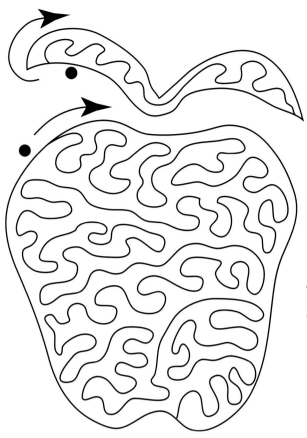

Apple and Leaves for Vest,
Peg Rack, Tissue Box, and
Tea Towel

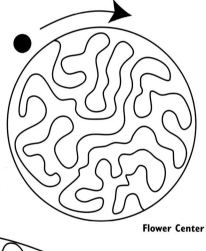

Flower for Blooming Posy Fleece Jacket
and Black-Eyed Susan Table Runner

Flower Center

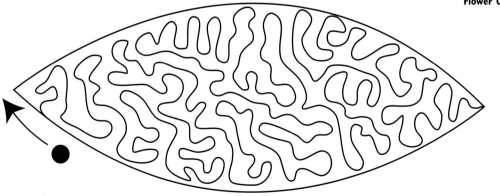

Petal

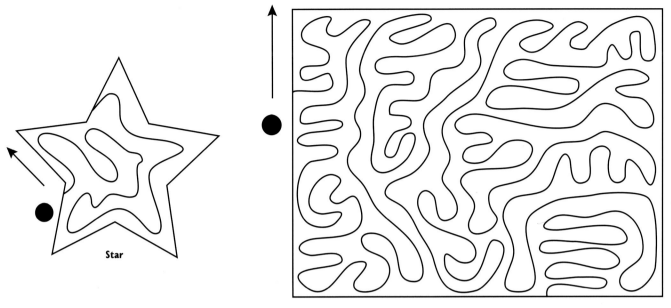

Star

Star Background

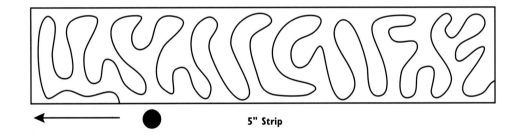

5" Strip

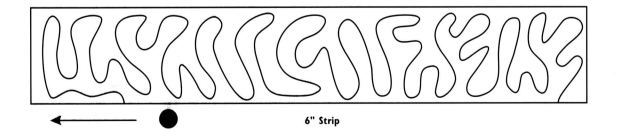

6" Strip

Flower and Leaves for Watercolor Jacket and Table Rug

Flower and Leaves for Table Rug, Watercolor Jacket, and Novelty Purse

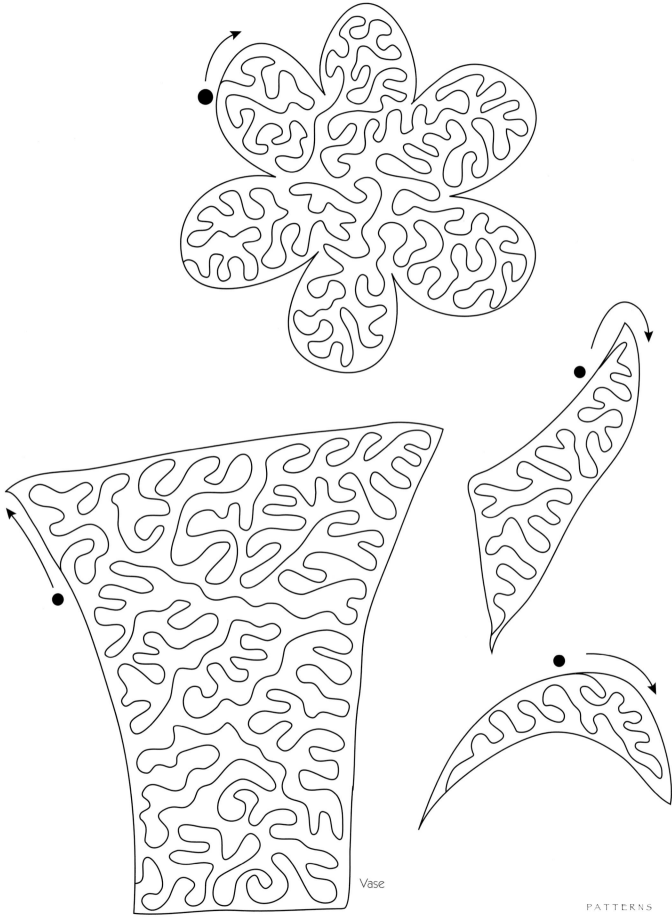

Vase

Flower and Flowerpot for Table Rug,
Watercolor Floral Jacket, and Sweet Kids Tulip

Flower for Flower
Wreath Pillow

Use this stem for
Novelty Purse and
Flower Wreath Pillow.

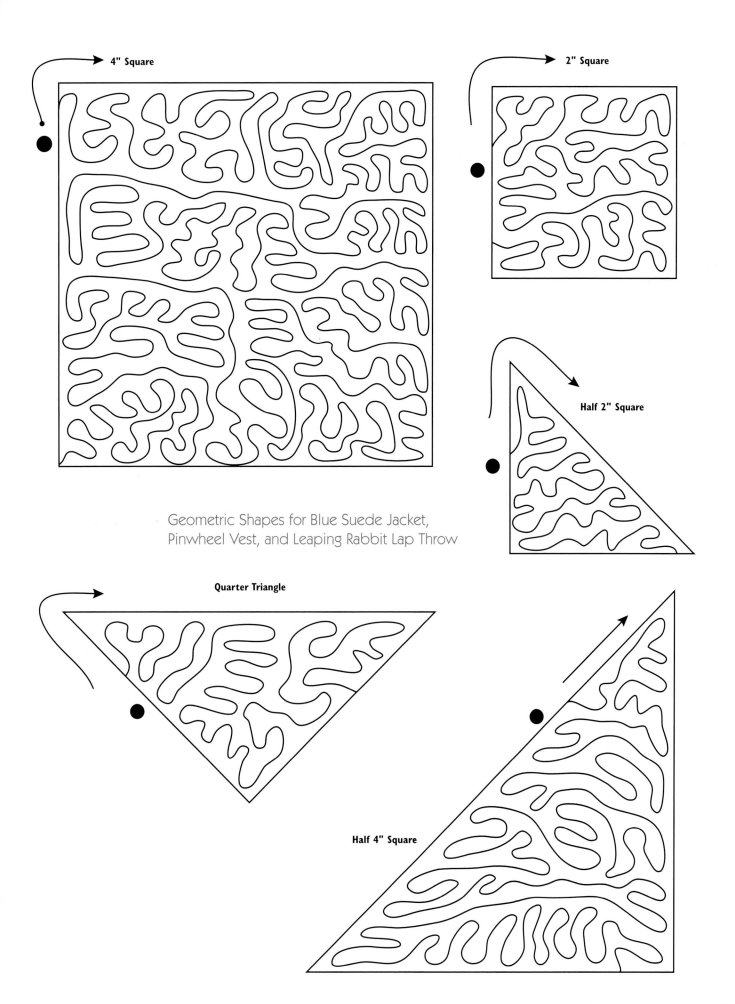

4" Square

2" Square

Half 2" Square

Geometric Shapes for Blue Suede Jacket,
Pinwheel Vest, and Leaping Rabbit Lap Throw

Quarter Triangle

Half 4" Square

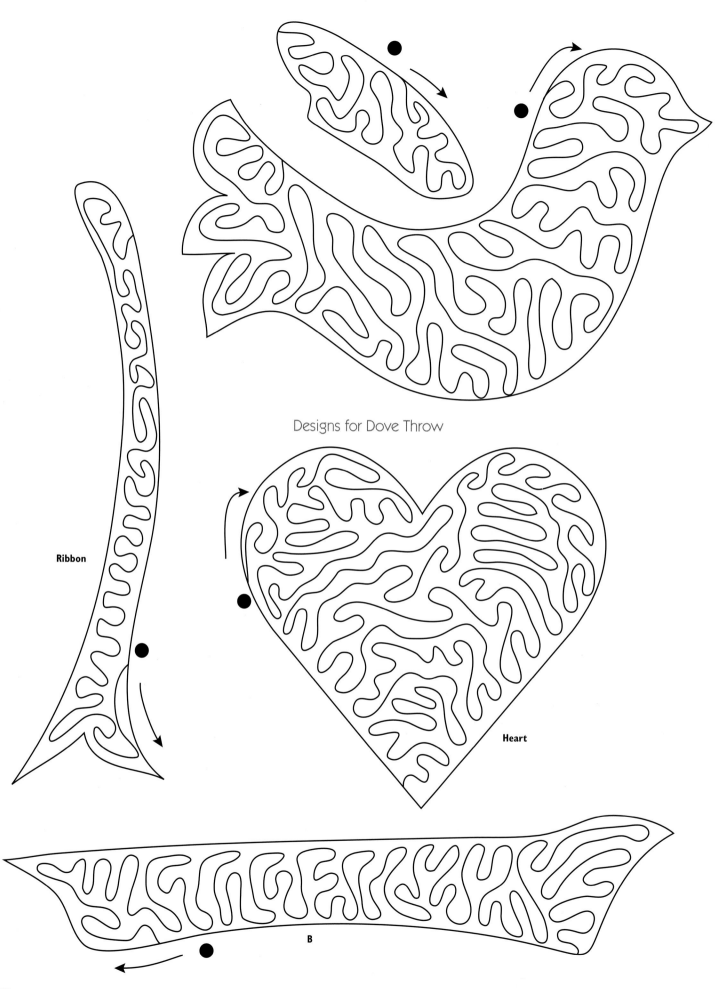

Designs for Dove Throw

Ribbon

Heart

B

Pumpkins for Wallhanging and Pillow

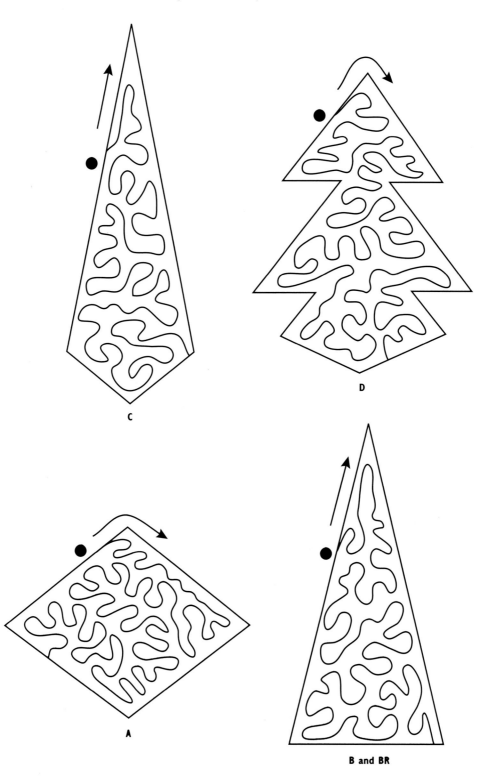

C

D

A

B and BR

Designs for Rabbit Projects

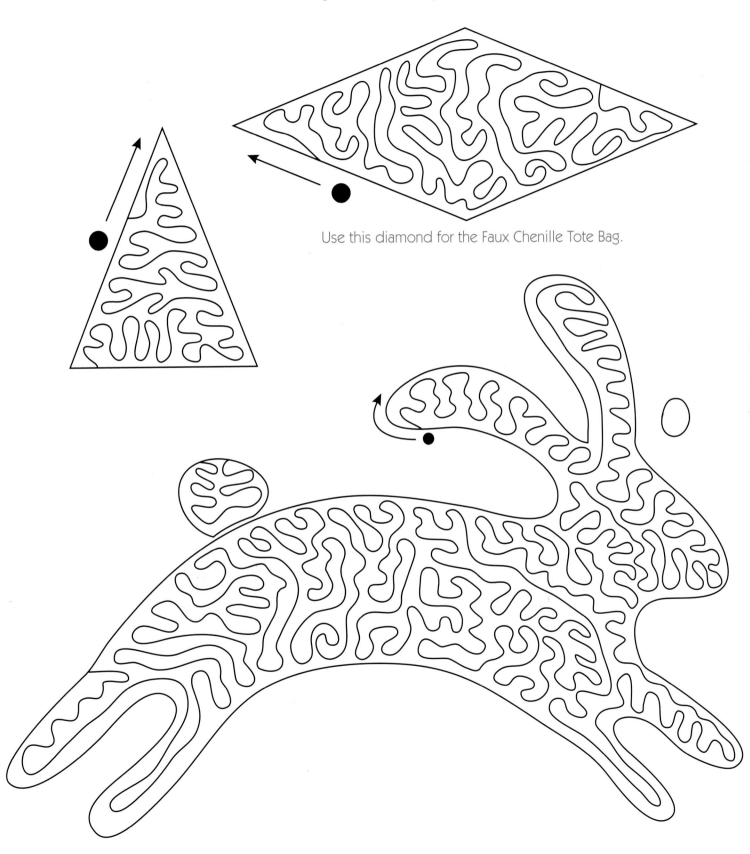

Use this diamond for the Faux Chenille Tote Bag.

Sweet Kids Designs

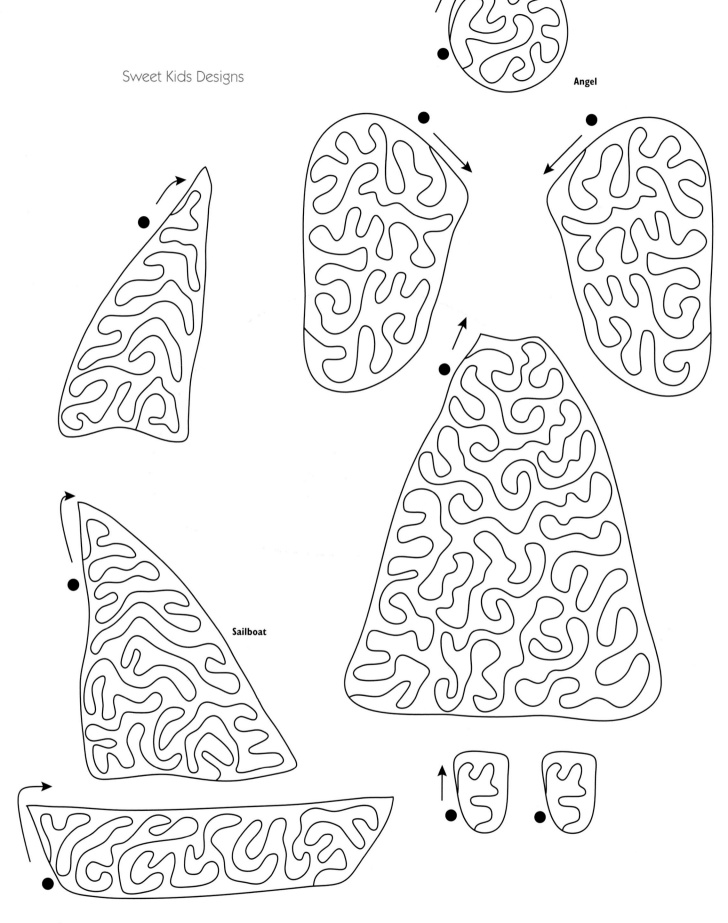

Angel

Sailboat

About the Author

Kathy MacMannis lives in Milford, Massachusetts, with her husband and three children. Raised in Redding, Connecticut, Kathy was surrounded by antiques and shared her family's passion for restoring colonial homes. A self-taught sewing and craft enthusiast since she was a small child, Kathy turned her love into a business. Five years ago, she ventured into the world of embroidery machine software and developed a technique that allowed her to manipulate the software programs to suit her specific needs. Her embroidery software expertise led to the beginning of KMAC Embroidery, which specializes in custom embroidery, and currently the Rag Wool Embroidery™ line.

Kathy created the Rag Wool Embroidery™ technique after a 2 a.m. inspiration; this technique allowed her to create the illusion of rug hooking on her embroidery machine. She has since published several design disks, and her designs can be found in national sewing and machine embroidery magazines. Kathy has taught at international sewing machine conventions, consumer expos, and as a freelance teacher around the country. Kathy was a recent guest on "America Sews."

Kathy graduated from Simmons College with a B.S. in nursing, and still works as an emergency room nurse at Milford Regional Hospital, Massachusetts.

Resources

KMAC Embroidery
8 Daniel R. Drive
Milford, MA 01757
(508) 478-9526
www.ragwool.com
100 percent wool, hand-dyed wool, pre-cut wool "cutlets", wooden embroidery hoops, patterns, Sulky® products, Triple "S" water-soluble stabilizer, and jacket pattern.

The Snap Source, Inc.
P.O. Box 99733
Troy, MI 48099
1-800-725-4600
www.snapsource.com

Plaid Enterprises
P.O. Box 7600
Norcross, GA 30091-7600
A source for crackle medium and other craft products.

Index

HOW TO USE THE DESIGNS ON THIS DISK

Insert the disk in your CD-Rom drive. When you open the drive, you will see individual project folders. Within each folder there will be individual format folders. Follow your manual to choose the folder that relates to your machine.

| CSD | EXP | DST | HUS/SHV |
| PCS | PES | SEW | JEF |

Included is free Adobe Acrobat Reader® so you can view the Read Me file. I strongly recommend that you read the complete Read Me File before you begin a project.
Refer to your owner's manual to transfer the designs from your computer to your embroidery machine.

Questions? Contact Kathy MacMannis
at 508-478-9526 or info@ragwool.com.

For more information write for a free catalog:

C&T Publishing, Inc.
P.O. Box 1456
Lafayette, CA 94549
(800) 284-1114
e-.   info@ctpub.com
Web   www.ctpub.com

For quilting supplies:
Cotton Patch Mail Order
3405 Hall Lane, Dept. CTB
Lafayette, CA 94549
(800) 835-4418
(925) 283-7883
e-mail: quiltusa@yahoo.com
Website: www.quiltusa.com